Peak Oil Survival

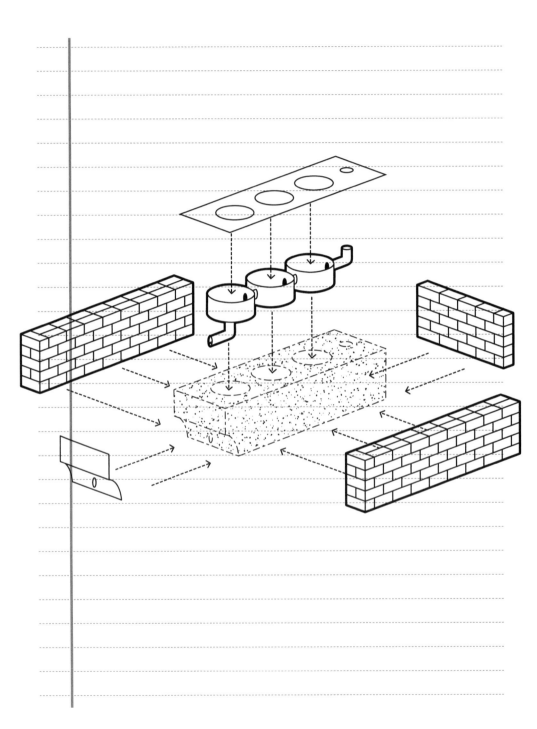

Peak Oil Survival:

PREPARATION FOR LIFE AFTER GRIDCRASH

Aric McBay

THE LYONS PRESS
Guilford, Connecticut
An imprint of The Globe Pequot Press

The Lyons Press is an imprint of The Globe Pequot Press.

10 9 8 7 6 5 4 3 2 1

Printed in the United States of America

ISBN-13: 978-1-59228-127-5
ISBN-10: 1-59228-127-3

Library of Congress Cataloging-in-Publication Data

McBay, Aric.
  Peak oil survival : preparation for life after gridcrash / Aric McBay.
    p. cm.
  ISBN-13: 978-1-59228-127-5
  ISBN-10: 1-59228-127-3
  I. Title.
  GF86.M34 2006
  613.6'9–dc22
                                        2006022138

CONTENTS

INTRODUCTION

WE LIVE IN AN AGE of converging crises. The depletion of freshwater supplies, the devastation of fish populations in the oceans, the destruction of topsoil, and growing climate change are just a few of the issues we face. Until this point, industrialized society has been able to deal with these issues by making use of cheap and widely available fossil fuels.

In essence, major ecological problems have been masked by cheap energy. Running out of water? No problem—drill a deeper well or build a pipeline and get water from elsewhere. Ninety percent of big ocean fish are wiped out? Just build a bigger net and trawl deeper and farther than ever. Losing topsoil? Just brew up some fertilizer with cheap natural gas and ship in food from a place where the farmland hasn't yet turned to desert. Warmer climate? Turn up the air-conditioning and get those diesel-powered bulldozers to toss a few extra buckets of soil on the levees to keep back those oceans a little longer.

But the crutch of cheap energy won't always be around. In fact, the consensus among retired and independent petroleum geologists is that the crutch is about to be yanked out—and soon.

PEAK OIL

That's because of something called *peak oil*, a phenomenon that has been recognized for half a century but is only now beginning to attract widespread public attention. Peak oil is really quite straightforward. It works like this: We know that there is a finite amount of oil on the planet and a finite number of oil fields. Each field has a finite life span, and oil extraction (or "production," as it is inaccurately called) follows a bell curve—minimal extraction at the beginning, maximum extraction in the middle, and minimal extraction at the end of the oil field's life span.

In 1956 a geophysicist named Marion King Hubbert extrapolated this curve to apply to all-time oil production. Hubbert originally predicted that oil would peak around the year 2000, but later geologists with more decades of data to assess extended that date to around the present day. We know that oil production follows the curve of oil field discovery by about forty years, and that the discovery of new oil fields peaked in the year 1965. Richard

Heinberg's book, *The Party's Over: Oil, War and the Fate of Industrial Societies,* is an excellent and current introduction to this subject, as is the highly readable book *Life After the Oil Crash* by Matt Savinar. Both authors recognize the severity of the peak oil situation and the seriousness of likely outcomes.

Unfortunately, most mainstream media coverage of peak oil has tended to downplay the seriousness and urgency of the problem, directing attention instead to superficial "techno-fixes." This is of special concern because, according to Kenneth Deffeyes of Princeton University, peak oil may have already occurred in late 2005. Although it will take a few years to confirm that assumption, credible, independent observers generally believe that production will peak within the next few years—if it hasn't already done so. From the peak onward there will be less and less oil available every year to fuel industrial civilization.

OTHER COMPLICATIONS

The peak oil situation is complicated by several factors. For one thing, the "easy" oil was mined first. Oil deposits closest to the surface and easiest to access—and those of the best quality ("sweet crude")—have largely been extracted. This means that the oil still in the ground is of lower quality, on average, than what's already been used. It also means that the remaining oil will take more effort and energy to extract and refine, because it must be drilled deeper and lifted a greater distance, and because it will take more crude to produce the same amount of some refined products like gasoline.

Another problem is that other fossil fuels, such as natural gas, will not necessarily have the same gradual decline as oil production. As Julian Darley observed in his book *High Noon for Natural Gas*, the production of natural gas may have a very sharp "cliff" in which gas production declines rapidly and without warning. It's estimated that Canada has less than an eight-year supply of natural gas remaining, and some countries like New Zealand are already seeing a rapid decline in production. Furthermore, natural gas is very difficult to move from one continent to another because of its volatility and the lack of capacity for ocean-going liquid natural gas (LNG) tankers. So once an area runs out of natural gas, it may be out of natural gas permanently.

Natural gas is especially important for running the basic infrastructure of industrial civilization. Natural gas serves as an energy source and "feedstock" for the manufacture of plastics, pesticides, and fertilizers. A decline in natural gas availability, or significant hikes due to shortages, would mean an end to many cheap plastics and a decline in agricultural production. Within the last several years, some agricultural fertilizer factories have already been forced to close due to increasing natural gas prices.

THE INADEQUACY OF RENEWABLES

But why not just switch seamlessly to renewable energy sources? Unfortunately for industrial civilization, many renewable energy sources have major drawbacks or impediments to implementation on a large scale.

One issue is "energy return on energy invested" (EROEI). To extract a barrel of oil from the ground requires a significant amount of energy. The energy costs (or energy invested) include the initial exploration to find and map the oil field, the building and maintaining of oil rigs, pumping the oil from deep underground, and transporting that oil via ship and pipeline to wherever it is going. The energy in that barrel of oil, minus the cost of getting it to a consumer, is the net energy yield, or the energy return on energy invested. Every source of energy requires an energy investment, whether it's building and maintaining solar panels and electrical infrastructures for solar energy, or mining, processing, and extracting uranium for nuclear power.

To adequately replace oil and maintain industrial society, an energy source would need to meet several main criteria:

> a) It must be possible to *scale up capacity rapidly* to compensate for oil production decline.
> b) It must have a *high energy return on energy invested.*
> c) It must be *transportable, storable, and energy-dense.* Oil carries a large amount of energy per unit of volume compared to alternatives like hydrogen. Additionally, the infrastructure to transport and store oil is already in place.
> d) It must be *renewable*, or it will only postpone the problem and possibly make it worse.
> e) It must be *ecologically sane.* An ecologically destructive energy source will not only decrease quality of life, but it will also create other energy and economic costs (such as the building of new water-treatment plants for contaminated water supplies).

As Heinberg and Savinar have written, no alternative source of energy meets all of these criteria.

In theory, **BIOFUELS** like biodiesel and ethanol could be scaled up to mass production. There is some debate about the EROEI of various biofuels, but it is certainly possible to produce net energy from at least some of them. Ethanol and biodiesel don't store as much energy per gallon as gasoline does, but the difference isn't astronomical, and they could use some of the same industrial infrastructure. The main problem is that biofuels require huge amounts of land to produce the farm crops that are turned into biofuels.

In fact, producing biofuels for the current U.S. automobile fleet would require turning the entire continental U.S. into a gigantic fuel farm, leaving no land on which to grow food, forests, or anything else. That's why English columnist George Monbiot has called biofuels "worse than fossil fuels" and "an ecological and humanitarian disaster." Every year, humans use 400 times as much energy as is captured by all of the plants on earth. That means that if one year's growth of every plant on the planet was turned into biofuels, it would still only produce one-quarter of 1 percent of the energy civilization uses every year.

Currently, many biodiesel enthusiasts make their fuel from used restaurant-fryer oil, which certainly does prevent some wastage. But there is only enough used fryer oil to supply a tiny fraction of the automobiles currently in use, and if oil supplies got very tight, that fryer oil would certainly not be available for general civilian use.

SOLAR POWER for electricity generation has inspired some debate over the issue of its EROEI. Some critics argue that building a solar panel currently requires more energy than it would give back over its entire lifetime of operation. Regardless of the current EROEI, it's certainly plausible that solar panels in the future will have an improved EROEI. However, implementing solar power on a large scale would require a swift and massive investment in the infrastructure at every level of society. Currently, political will for this is lacking, partly because the expense of building that infrastructure would not be repaid for many years.

Any system that generates electricity has other shortcomings as well. Specifically, electricity does not provide the carbon that natural gas does as a feedstock for the production of agricultural chemicals and plastics, since plastics and pesticides are physically made from the carbon in fossil fuels. In addition, electricity cannot be transported and stored with the ease of oil. To meet current energy demands with only electricity would require creating additional power lines to transport the energy, as well as batteries or other facilities to store the energy. Doing this on a large scale would essentially require building a whole new industrial infrastructure in a time of energy decline.

WIND POWER is likely the most promising source of renewable energy. It has the best EROEI of any of the alternative power sources. However, scaling up wind generation rapidly would prove challenging. Richard Heinberg notes that meeting only 18 percent of current U.S. energy consumption would require building 200,000 state-of-the-art wind turbines every single year for the next twenty-seven years, and that wind turbine factories globally are only producing about one-fifth of that number each year. Additionally, a growing population would mean that energy demand by that time would significantly exceed current demand. Wind power has the same shortcomings as any energy source that generates only electricity.

NUCLEAR POWER has been touted recently as a solution to all energy woes, but a closer inspection reveals that the situation isn't so sunny. According to a recent U.S. Army report,[1] the worldwide supplies of "low-cost uranium" will be exhausted in about twenty years if current trends continue. According to the UN International Atomic Energy Agency, all uranium (low-cost or not) will be exhausted in about fifty years if current trends continue. Of course, a major decline in oil extraction would increase the use of uranium, meaning that those estimates are far too optimistic. But the issue of scale is the major problem. About 450 nuclear plants have been built in the past fifty years worldwide. To meet global energy requirements for the year 2030 would require building at least 520 new plants every year. That would mean building more plants every single year than in all of human history, and doing so with declining oil availability. Even optimistic observers suggest that fusion power with net energy production is at least fifty years in the future (assuming it is ever developed). Again, nuclear power has the same shortcomings as any energy source that generates only electricity.

HYDROELECTRIC DAMS are already widespread, but in many countries (including the U.S.), dams have already been built on almost all the large rivers that can be dammed. In other words, it would be difficult to increase hydroelectric generation capacity much beyond its current level in most regions. In terms of environmental impact, dams destroy habitat when their reservoirs are created and ruin streams or dry up rivers upon which those downstream depend.

In some Third World areas where dams are still being constructed, dams have had a horrendous humanitarian impact, with governments using military or paramilitary forces to violently displace millions of people at a time. In addition—and this may come as a surprise—dams can produce huge amounts of greenhouse gases. When the dam reservoirs are formed, they trap large amounts of organic matter underwater. As this matter is broken down through decomposition, the carbon is released in the form of greenhouse gases for many decades. A study of dams in Brazil showed that hydroelectric dams released nearly thirteen times as much greenhouse gas as a coal plant would to generate the same amount of electricity. Once again, hydroelectric power has the same shortcomings as any energy source that generates only electricity.

HYDROGEN POWER, FUEL CELLS, AND SIMILAR DEVICES will not adequately replace fossil fuels because they are not sources of energy; they can only store and transport energy that has already been generated from another method. In fact, these devices actually use extra energy because of the energy needed to build and maintain their infrastructure, as well as the energy that is always lost when energy is converted from one form (like electricity) to another (like hydrogen).

---

1 http://www.usnews.com/usnews/news/articles/060315/15natsec.htm

Many sources of renewable energy can provide good transitional or buffering solutions on a community scale. However, no source can be scaled up to a level that would maintain industrial civilization.

EFFECTS AND CONSEQUENCES

It's hard to overstate the seriousness of the situation. Almost every single aspect of modern life is dependent on cheap and abundant fossil fuels.

Take **FOOD**: Industrial farming is highly energy-intensive, requiring vast amounts of energy to synthesize pesticides and fertilizers. More importantly, that food is transported great distances from where it is grown. Richard Manning notes in *The Oil We Eat* that for every calorie of energy we get from food, approximately 10 calories of oil energy are consumed. This means that if the current system of industrial agriculture had to be energy-self-sufficient, it would produce less than 10 percent of the food that it currently does. That's just an average, and meat production requires much more energy. Pork production, for example, consumes 68 calories for every food calorie created. To make food without fossil fuels, we actually must net more food calories than the energy we expend, and that means radically restructuring how we produce food.

Everyday **CONSUMABLE GOODS,** disposable products, plastics, and pharmaceuticals are all energy-intensive to manufacture and are frequently shipped great distances overseas, which is also energy-expensive. As energy availability declines, such products will become more expensive, and some will become impossible to obtain.

TRANSPORTATION is almost completely and directly dependent on fossil fuels. This goes for the transportation of people as well as goods. It's possible for mass transit, car pooling, and reduced automobile use to slightly delay the effects of oil depletion on transport. However, most energy used for transportation goes toward moving goods, not commuters. Also, building more gas-efficient new vehicles is not as much of a solution as it seems, because most of the energy expended in a vehicle's lifetime is used during that vehicle's manufacture. That means building a brand-new, gas-efficient car can take up much more energy than simply fixing up an older car. Also, because hybrid or battery-powered cars are more complex to build, use energy-intensive high-tech and lightweight materials, and require more maintenance (such as the regular replacement of batteries), they require more energy to build than gas-powered vehicles. One recent study showed that hybrid vehicles were actually less energy-efficient than gas-guzzling SUVs over their respective lifetimes, because hybrid vehicles require such a large amount of energy to manufacture.[2]

----

2   See the "Dust to Dust" study at http://cnwmr.com/nss-folder/automotiveenergy/. To see a perspective critiquing the study, visit http://thewatt.com/modules.php? name=News&file=article&thold=-1&mode=nested&order=1&sid=1070.

INTERNATIONAL POLITICS AND WARFARE definitely cause grave concern in terms of the peak oil situation. As the demand for oil supplies continues to increase, some nations will take (and currently are taking) violent measures to ensure that they have control of as much oil as possible. Because their economies will collapse without oil, many government leaders may believe they have nothing to lose, and subsequently go to extreme lengths to obtain oil, as well as freshwater and other substances likely to be in tighter supply in the future. It's hard to tell what form this conflict might take, but most peak oil observers seem to agree that resource wars will become a defining aspect of the next several decades.

FINANCES AND ECONOMICS are major issues as well. As Matt Savinar discussed in *Life After the Oil Crash*, the modern economy is completely dependent on perpetual growth. This is largely because of interest rates, which demand that more things be bought and sold each year to repay loans and investors. However, a decline in oil production will mean a decline in manufacturing and product transportation, which will consequently lead to a decline in employment and, eventually, widespread economic collapse. The situation is complicated by the fact that the stock market is entirely based on faith that the current economic system will continue indefinitely and that investments will be repaid. If collapse appeared imminent, investors would pull their money out of the stock market, meaning that even the likelihood of impending economic collapse would itself cause economic collapse.

ELECTRICAL GRIDS are also dependent on cheap fossil fuels. They are also highly vulnerable and require close attention and constant maintenance. For example, the massive blackout in North America in August 2003 was caused merely by numerous tree branches touching major power lines in several different places.

Various aspects of the industrial infrastructure are highly interdependent. Electrical grids need to function in order for fuel and gas pipelines to operate, which is one reason why Hurricane Katrina caused fuel shortages in some areas (when the pipelines shut down). Conversely, many electrical grids use natural gas as a major source of energy for power generation. Furthermore, telecommunications grids are becoming dependent on the electrical grid as well. Historically, phone lines were copper wires that could carry electricity from phone company generators in the event of an outage. Those lines are now being switched over to fiber-optic systems, which require electricity at both the transmitting and receiving ends. The point of all this is that each part of the grid is dependent on the smooth functioning of other parts of the grid. If one major sector of the grid goes down, it can cause the other parts to fail in a cascading systems crash. Unfortunately, the dominant economic and political systems reward short-term, rather than long-term, approaches. By the time politicians and business leaders become seriously aware of the severity of our situation, many opportunities will have been missed. And, paradoxically, as discussed above, the awareness of business leaders could very well trigger economic collapse as people attempt to move capital out of banks and stock markets and into useful physical objects and supplies.

ECOLOGICAL COLLAPSE

All of these outcomes are likely to occur against a background of ecological devastation. As mentioned before, cheap oil masks the effects of this devastation for those of us in the industrialized world. It is also cheap oil that permits most of this destruction to occur.

Perhaps you've heard that the oceans are in a state of ecological collapse. You may know that the population of large fish in the ocean has declined by 90 percent in the past fifty years, and that those remaining are significantly smaller.[3] And phytoplankton, the basis of the biosphere, has decreased in global population by 6 percent in a mere two decades, and by as much as 30 percent in some areas.[4] Populations of krill, the tiny animals just above phytoplankton on the oceanic food chain, are down by 80 percent in three decades.[5] You've probably read in the news that global warming will kill up to 37 percent of all species on earth by 2050 (and you may have noticed that estimates of these casualties from global warming seem to increase just about every week).[6] Even if you only pay attention to mainstream media, you can't help but notice that the living world is being ever more rapidly destroyed.

This ecological destruction also causes direct effects on human beings. More than one billion people lack access to potable water, and this water scarcity may impact as many as two-thirds of the world's population by the year 2025. Because of this, about 80 percent of illness worldwide is caused by bad water. This is worsened by global warming, as is land desertification, which threatens the ability of people in many parts of the world to produce enough food for themselves.

Cheap fossil fuels drive greenhouse gas emission and allow for the construction of dams and factories that take drinking water away from humans and other living creatures. The decreasing availability of oil will certainly not stop ecological destruction, but it will significantly reduce the ability of any one person or group to do that damage. Perhaps most crucially, it could

---

3   Myers, R. A. et al. (2003) "Rapid worldwide depletion of predatory fish communities" *Nature* 423, 280-283, *Letters to Nature*

4   Gregg, W. W., and M. E. Conkright (2002) "Decadal changes in global ocean chlorophyll" *Geophys. Res. Lett.*, 29(15), 1730

5   Atkinson, A. et al. (2004) "Long-term decline in krill stock and increase in salps within the Southern Ocean" *Nature* 432, 100-103, *Letters to Nature*

6   Thomas, C. D. et al. (2004) "Extinction risk from climate change" *Nature* 427, 145-148, *Letters to Nature*.

prevent a "runaway greenhouse effect." It's a growing opinion among climate scientists that global warming beyond a certain critical point would become massive and self-perpetuating, regardless of industrial emissions beyond that point, and many scientists believe that we are now very close to that point.

INDUSTRIAL CIVILIZATION AND INDUSTRIAL COLLAPSE

The problems we face are not superficial. They are not caused by the kind of car you or I drive, by whether we buy recycled paper or not, by which politician we vote for, or by where we work. Certainly those things can affect the severity of the various issues, and how the next few decades play out, but they are not the fundamental cause. We can't solve the problems we face by simply changing those personal choices.

That's because these problems reach deeply into the foundation of society— into the very roots of civilization. I'm not using the word *civilization* to describe a society that is "refined, safe, convenient, modern, advanced, polite, enlightened, and sophisticated," as the dictionary defines it. Rather, I am using an anthropological definition of civilization that looks at the structure and functioning of a society rather than at the words people in that society use to flatter themselves (or to insult those living outside of civilization, such as by calling them "savages").[7]

For a more unbiased definition of civilization, we can consider historian Lewis Mumford's use of the word "to denote the group of institutions that first took form under kingship. Its chief features, constant in varying proportions throughout history, are the centralization of political power, the separation of classes, the lifetime division of labor, the mechanization of production, the magnification of military power, the economic exploitation of the weak, and the universal introduction of slavery and forced labor for both industrial and military purposes."[8] Anthropologist Stanley Diamond cuts to the chase, and says simply that "Civilization originates in conquest abroad and repression at home."[9]

Since their inception, civilizations (as opposed to land-based and sustainable indigenous groups) have created massive ecological destruction and have eventually destroyed themselves. Perhaps the most universal characteristic of historical civilizations is that they have all either collapsed or been conquered and engulfed by another civilization, which itself subsequently collapsed. Excellent books on this subject include *A Green History of the*

---

7   For an expansion of the discussion about the definition of civilization, visit
    http://inthewake.org/civdef.html.
8   Mumford, Lewis. *The Myth of the Machine: Technics and Human Development*, Harcourt
    Brace Jovanovich, New York, 1966. Page 186.
9   Diamond, Stanley. *In Search of the Primitive: A Critique of Civilization*, Transaction
    Publishers, New Brunswick, 1993. Page 1.

World: The Environment and the Collapse of Great Civilizations by Clive Ponting, and the even more applicable *The Final Empire: The Collapse of Civilization and the Seed of the Future* by William H. Kotke.[10]

What these and other researchers have shown is that historical civilizations tend to expand their territory and resource exploitation as much as they can. This is a process motivated primarily by the short-term self-interest of those in power, who are rewarded with territory, resources, money, and slaves (or workers). The people in charge persistently make decisions that undermine the long-term sustainability of their civilization in order to increase their power, such as harvesting more trees or farming more intensively than is possible on a long-term, sustainable basis. Civilization is highly competitive, so if those in power aren't willing to make decisions that provide short-term gain (even if in the process, sustainability is undermined), someone else will be there to take their place.

For example, since farming too intensively damages the soil and eventually hurts crops, any civilization that has started over-intensive farming must intensify its farming even further just to maintain the same yields. Usually it will do this by increasing the complexity and energy demands of the farming process (like using synthetic fertilizers instead of compost), which then creates a vicious cycle of perpetual intensification. This vicious cycle occurs in every civilized endeavor, not just in agriculture. Historically, technical, ecological, financial, or social limitations have eventually prevented any given civilization from further increasing and intensifying production. This is the point at which civilizations collapse.

This process cannot be changed by electing new politicians, because politicians who try to get out of this cycle will cause what is likely to be perceived as short-term damage to an economy or to people's comfort, and will thus become very unpopular. Because of this, I believe that the only effective solution is to deal with the system itself.

What makes current civilizations different from earlier ones is that they are industrial. By industrial, I mean a society that is dependent on machines for the basics of life. A society that needs tractors to grow food, trucks to transport it, factories to synthesize fertilizers, and so on, is an industrial society. A society where people participate in the growing of their own food and other basics by hand would not be termed industrial.

Industrial civilization still has all of the same fundamental characteristics as those earlier civilizations, and its reliance on high technology does not exempt it from the previous patterns of decline. Indeed, technology has rapidly accelerated the expansion and destructiveness of our current civilization, and will likely accelerate the collapse as well. Because the industrial

----

10   The Final Empire can be read online in its entirety at www.rainbowbody.net/Finalempire/.

infrastructure is so complicated and interdependent, failure in one area can cause the whole system to fail, as discussed above. In our case, the rapid depletion of fossil fuels is likely to be a driving factor in this collapse because those fuels are required to operate the industrial machinery.

We are left in something of a catch-22. We know that in a post-collapse context, our well-being will depend on the well-being of the natural world, since we will once again be directly dependent on the ecological communities in our area. Most of us are currently dependent on industrial civilization for the material basis of our day-to-day lives. And yet, in the long term, every day that industrial civilization continues is another day that global warming worsens, that more rivers are dammed, depleted, or poisoned, that more fish are removed from the oceans, and that more forests are cut down.

How do we deal with this conflict between our long-term survival and our immediate comfort? I think that the answer is twofold. First, we must gather together in our communities and develop skills to meet our own needs. We must do this even as we work to disentangle ourselves and others from dependence on the global economy and industrial civilization.

Second, we must prevent industrial civilization from destroying our long-term ability to survive and thrive. If massive greenhouse gas emissions and other ecological catastrophes continue, our prospects will grow increasingly dim, no matter how well we can organize ourselves on a local scale. The first approach cannot succeed unless the second does. I believe it's up to us as small, face-to-face groups (the only groups that can really be democratic or accountable, in my opinion) to do what needs to be done to ensure that things turn out as well as possible.

For some it can be shocking, upsetting, or depressing to recognize that civilization is going to collapse, and there is nothing that can be done to stop it. However, there are constructive things that people can do, both during and after the collapse, and that is the focus of this book. Collapse—in theory, at least—doesn't necessarily have to be violent, and it could ideally involve less deprivation and poverty than now exist. But this would require an honest look at the situation by masses of people. It would mean scaling down industrial capacity as rapidly as possible and focusing efforts on ensuring that the basic survival needs of a large number of people are met on a local scale.

FINDING DEEPER SOLUTIONS

When I was a child my parents would often take me hiking and camping in the hills of the Canadian Shield, north of Lake Superior. It was there that I gained firsthand experience of what it's truly like to be in the wilderness, something that relatively few people get the chance to do. In my teenage years my parents sometimes had to drag me out camping with them, but in retrospect, I'm glad they did, because it fostered my enduring love for living creatures.

Much of my environmental consciousness grew during the late 1980s, in what was perhaps the heyday of mainstream environmentalism in North America. I worked on recycling and waste-reduction programs, and encouraged people to use reusable containers, to compost, and to bike instead of drive cars. At the time, it looked like the environmental movement was gaining steam so quickly that it couldn't possibly fail.

And, at the same time, scientists were warning that things had to change in the next decade, or it would be "too late." I began doing a lot of reading about ecology and the changes in our environment, so I saw that their warnings were completely valid. I presumed that this was so obvious, and environmentalism was becoming so popular, that plenty would change before the deadlines passed.

But a decade later I saw that very little had changed. Indeed, most indicators of environmental health had gotten dramatically worse rather than better. What was going wrong? How had the environmental movement experienced such lackluster success at such a critical time? More to the point, I began to ask myself, should I give up on an approach that clearly wasn't working and try to find one that would?

These things take time to understand, because often the biggest obstacles to comprehension are emotional rather than rational. Fortunately, my attachment to traditional styles of mainstream environmental organizing was exceeded by my love for the land, and by my desire to preserve drinkable water for current and future populations, and to safeguard the health of ecological systems on which food sources (such as fish) depend. These concerns led me to search for the deeper roots of our current problems, and for deeper solutions, which I eventually found in a critique of civilization.

I had come across information about peak oil several years before my thinking shifted in this new direction. But it wasn't until four or five years after my initial exposure, and after continued reading and research, that I started to understand the seriousness and extent of the implications of peak oil.

While I was thinking about these things, I spent much of my time working on social-justice and environmental projects. As I did so, I came to understand that much of the progress we did make could easily be washed away by peak oil and ecological collapse. I grew worried that governments and societies would swiftly abandon their already-limited efforts to help marginalized people and the living world in favor of more immediate physical and economic self-preservation.

In recent years, my focus has again shifted somewhat. For example, I've learned how to grow my own food, and how to forage wild edibles from the area where I live. Working within community gardens, ecological food-growing cooperatives, and the like, I am able to share that knowledge with others and to learn more. Most of all, I'm striving for "community sufficiency" rather than "self-sufficiency." Much of my work now revolves around building communities with an interest in social justice and environmentalism, which are also skilled and robust enough to thrive even during major economic, ecological, and social disruption. I hope that those communities will act as a template for others. My writing has been an outgrowth of all these efforts.

THE PURPOSE OF THIS BOOK

This book is about far more than just peak oil. And it's about more than mere survival. This book is a primer designed to help communities deal with problems we will face in the near future, as well as a handbook for people who want to live "off the grid" now.

This book is part of a larger project called *In the Wake: A Collective Manual-in-Progress for Outliving Civilization*. This project, and my writings and life in general, are based on the premise that industrial civilization is destroying the living world. I want to help create communities that are equitable, ecologically sound, and sustainable. I also believe that we can't do this within the machinery of industrial civilization. Many of us are very busy with making a living, taking care of ourselves and each other, and generally trying to fix problems in our own parts of the world. We can't all spend as much time as we'd like camping in the forest, growing gardens, taking wilderness first-aid classes, or learning other survival skills to prepare for collapse. It is important to note, however, that the likely timeline for collapse is staggeringly short. According to some observers, we can expect massive disruptions of global industrial and transportation systems starting as early as 2010.[11] One reason that I am writing this is to create a "crash course" for the crash, a way of quickly introducing a variety of important skills and technologies to people who aren't familiar with them, as well as to provide a reference and resource for those who are.

It's difficult to predict exactly how the impending collapse may play out. Various civilizations in history took many years (even decades) to collapse. So, looking at those examples, it's tempting to go back to sleep, saying, "Don't worry; we have plenty of time to figure out how to deal with collapse. It will happen gradually." But that's far from guaranteed. Those civilizations took centuries or millennia to reach their full extent. The dominant technological civilization on the planet is dependent on machines that are only decades old. The time-scale of change has been profoundly compressed by rapid industrial change. We can expect the rate of collapse to reflect that compression. Also, those historical civilizations were based on technologies that were much less interdependent than ours. If the oil supply is interrupted, it becomes impossible to maintain the electrical generation and distribution infrastructure. If the electrical infrastructure fails, then almost all of the rest of the infrastructure shuts down immediately. Telecommunications may continue temporarily

---

11   **Duncan, Richard C.,** *Olduvai Cliff Revisited: The Olduvai Cliff Event:* **a.** *2007,* **March 5, 2001. (see online at www.mnforsustain.org/oil_duncan_r_olduvai_cliff_revisited.htm)**

by generator and battery power, but even communications are becoming electrically dependent, and hence, more brittle.

Additionally, there is reason to believe that industrial collapse may happen very rapidly because of deliberate attacks on industrial infrastructures—oil and electrical infrastructures in particular. These attacks are quite common in some areas of the world, and are increasing in North America.[12] If there was a coordinated attempt to collapse the industrial system by a small group of committed people, near-total industrial collapse could happen very quickly, over a period of weeks, or even days.

Though it may seem ironic to some, I believe that this rapid collapse is probably the "best-case scenario" for the planet. I'm a bit of an optimist, despite the awful state of things. So I'm planning for an optimistic scenario that involves near-term, rapid industrial collapse. It's a remote possibility that industrial civilization may continue for decades longer if it makes extensive use of coal and certain last-ditch, ecologically insane energy sources. But if it does last that long, our prospects are very grim. I doubt that many, if any, human beings would survive, let alone most other species. And I'm not going to write a book for a world with no humans in it—who would read it? So that leaves us with the urgency of a book for the "optimistic" scenario of rapid collapse.

The techniques covered in this book are based on the following general criteria:

- They apply broadly and generally to a variety of bioregions, or have the potential to be exceptionally beneficial to people in some bioregions.

- They permit a reduced impact and/or reduced consumption, rather than increasing consumption.

- They operate with "found resources" and remnant resources as much as possible, as opposed to cultivation or metal working, in order to maintain existing wild areas and minimize labor.

- The techniques are relatively simple so they can be learned quickly.

---

12 For more general and continuing information on infrastructure attacks and insurgency, see John Robb's site at http://globalguerrillas.typepad.com/. For specific information on infrastructure in Iraq, see http://www.iags.org/iraqpipelinewatch.htm. For information on recent events in Nigeria, see http://en.wikipedia.org/wiki/Nigerian_Oil_Crisis and http://en.wikipedia.org/wiki/MEND.

- They are as compact as possible, to maintain existing wild areas. (A technique that allows a 1,000-square-foot garden to meet food needs would generally be preferred to a 1,500-square-foot garden that yields the same amount of food, since the smaller garden leaves more room for wilderness. This assumes that both gardens are equally sustainable.)

- They rely on items that are easy to find or make, so as to permit democratic application and reduced scarcity.

- Whenever possible, their use is creative and fulfilling, rather than repetitive.

- They are portable, and able to be expanded or scaled up rapidly

- It's possible for a small group to build and maintain the tools and equipment involved.

- Wherever possible, their use calls for the degradation of remnants of the industrial system and the rejuvenation of the land.

- The techniques chosen tend to make societies more egalitarian and to distribute resources and power more fairly.

I hope that this information is useful to you. If you have any comments or suggestions, or wish to contribute to the project, please do contact us. You can also check out the website at www.inthewake.org, or e-mail me at editorial@ inthewake.org. There you can see more information about the project, more discussion and essays, additional links to web pages and books of interest, as well as more information about relevant skills and strategies. There I provide a resource not just to help people survive industrial collapse, but also to share some of the skills people will need to stop industrial civilization from destroying our long-term prospects, and for people to build egalitarian and ecological communities of their own.

Thanks for your interest, and good skill to you.

ACKNOWLEDGMENTS

Many thanks to the following individuals for their proofreading, comments, and suggestions: MM, Tammy T., Melissa, Edward, Emily, Andrea, Pig Monkey, Wabbit, Lori, Ken McWatters, and several anonymous contributors. Thanks also to the many people who offered supportive comments and feedback.

Thank you to Alex for the illustration on page 52, and to Jen for those on pages 3 and 17.

The drawings on pages 8 and 9 are based on those from the *Sourcebook of Alternative Technologies for Freshwater Augmentation in Small Island Developing States* (available at www.unep.or.jp.). The illustration on page 21 is based on a version from Handout #655 published by the RYAN Foundation.

On page 23, Figure 10b: Lightweight Solar Still is based on a design from the excellent *Survival Scrapbook, Volume Two: Access to Tools* by Dave Williams and Stephanie Munro (Schocken Books, 1973).

On page 78, Figure 34: Improvised Oil Lamp is based on a design in Cresson Kearney's *Nuclear War Survival Skills* (Oregon Institute of Science & Medicine, 4th Rep edition 1999).

In creating this book, I used free, open-source software, including the text editor Vim, the word processor Open Office, the vector drawing application Inkscape, the raster image editing application GIMP, and the desktop publishing program Scribus.

A NOTE ON REFERENCES

The information in this book represents an amalgamation of my own experience and that of other contributors, as well as material from print and online sources listed. General references on a chapter subject are listed at the end of that chapter. References that apply to a specific subtopic are listed at the end of respective sections of a chapter.

PART 1

Obtaining Water

CHAPTER 1

WATER FOR SURVIVAL AND SAFETY

GAINING ACCESS TO SUFFICIENT WATER is the most crucial issue individuals face in a survival situation. People with no drinkable water can die in as little time as three days. How much water do you need? According to the United Nations, the "absolute survival minimum" is just less than two gallons (7 liters) per person per day for drinking and wash water. Some sources list minimal drinking-water requirements as low as 2 to 3 quarts (or liters) per person per day for a healthy person in cool weather, without strenuous physical exercise. However, significant health problems may result from drinking such small quantities for a prolonged period of time. Normally, your body extracts water from the food you eat, so if you are eating less, you must compensate by drinking more water.

In a shortage situation, try to provide at least 4 to 5 gallons (15 to 20 liters) of water per person per day for drinking and washing. People who are ill may need more. Wash water is needed to avert serious health problems caused by infections and disease. If you cannot achieve that level with water that is safe for drinking, also called potable water, you can use non-potable, brackish, or salty water for some wash purposes. However, you should purify water used for washing the face or hands, or for brushing teeth.

In a water shortage, avoid alcohol and caffeine, and never drink blood, urine, or salty water, as drinking those liquids would only increase your water requirements. Also, if you have an extremely small drinking-water supply, consider minimizing your protein intake, since protein requires water to digest. If you have no water, you should not eat at all.

When you are getting by on a limited supply of water, watch for signs of dehydration. Indicators include extreme thirst; dark, sunken eyes; low urine output; dark urine with a very strong odor; fatigue; loss of skin elasticity; a "trench line" down the center of the tongue; and emotional instability. If you are in a survival situation without other sources of water, digging a well for water is usually not worth the energy expenditure and depletion of sweat.

CONTAMINATION

It doesn't matter how much water you have if that water is too contaminated for drinking. Contamination of water can be pathogenic, chemical, or physical.

Pathogenic organisms are "disease-causing organisms," so pathogenic contamination refers to the presence of certain types of bacteria, amoebas, worms, or viruses. Giardiasis (or "beaver fever") and cholera are two illnesses caused by pathogens.

Chemical contamination includes contamination from pesticides and industrial chemicals, or natural chemicals from rocks. Toxic pesticides include DDT and methyl bromide. Salts and iron are natural chemicals that can prove harmful in certain situations. (Of course, if you were a fish living in the ocean, you wouldn't consider salt a "contaminant," so the issue of toxicity is relative.)

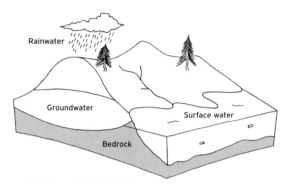

FIGURE 1: WATER TYPES

Physical contaminants are not usually harmful, but can make the water unappealing to drink because of taste, color, or smell. "Cloudiness," also known as turbidity, is one example.

Avoiding water contamination in the first place is always preferable to having to treat water. In almost every conceivable situation, it is easier to keep water clean than to clean it. There are three main sources of water: groundwater, rainwater, and surface water. Each type will be discussed, along with other survival sources of water that don't fit into these categories.

| GROUNDWATER

GROUNDWATER, AS THE NAME IMPLIES, is present below the surface of the ground. This primarily includes water obtained from wells and springs. As water flows through the ground, it is filtered and purified by the soil. The United Nations considers groundwater the preferred source of water in refugee situations. A spring is considered the ideal source of groundwater, since you don't have to dig a well to gain access to it. Groundwater is generally free of pathogens; however, contamination can occur from latrines that are located too close to a water source.

ABOUT WELLS

A well is simply a hole dug or drilled down to the level of the groundwater. Locating an appropriate site for a well can be a challenge, especially since hand-digging a well is very labor-intensive, and you don't want to spend time and effort digging a dry well.

If there is a dry season where you are, try to dig the well at the end of it. That's when the groundwater level is the lowest. If you dig when the groundwater is high, it will move down in dryer weather, leaving your well dry. One indicator of a potentially good well site is the presence of healthy, green vegetation. Look for evergreen plants that grow where water is close to the surface, like willow and cedar. Plants that come and go with the seasons, such as most ferns, are less-reliable indicators.

When siting a well, try to find a place where the water table is as close as possible to the surface, so that your well will be easy to dig, but also where the water table is deep, so that seasonal variations will not dry your well. Consult hydrological and topographical maps for your area. Such maps may be found at local government offices or libraries (especially those at universities). They can also be ordered in the U.S. from the United States Geological Survey (http://topomaps.usgs.gov/), or in Canada from Natural Resources Canada's Centre for Topographic Information (http://maps.nrcan.gc.ca/index_e.php).

You can also place a well near a river, but it should be at least 50 feet (15 meters) from a riverbank. Such a well will be "recharged" by the river water as it gradually percolates through and is purified by the soil. However, never place a well where it may be flooded by surface water, which could cause contamination.

Wells should never be dug near latrines, rubbish dumps, or animal pens. Try to leave a distance of at least 100 feet (30 meters) from these potential sources of groundwater pollution. Wells should be at least 330 feet (100 meters) from possible sources of industrial pollution.

There are several techniques for digging wells. I will describe the one that is most appropriate for an improvised situation. Among the methods for digging or drilling a well, some require installing a pipe and a hand-pump to operate, which is beyond the scope of this book.

For information on well-drilling techniques, see *WELL Technical Brief #43: Simple Drilling Methods,* available at www.lboro.ac.uk/well/resources/technical-briefs/technical-briefs.htm. You can also refer to D. V. Allen's website, www.consallen.com/hand_drilling.htm for more information.

DIGGING A WELL

The basic method for creating an improvised well is to simply dig a hole in the ground. A diameter of at least 4 feet (1.2 meters) is needed for two people digging together. The United Nations Environment Programme (UNEP) suggests digging a well with a height-to-width ratio of 2:1. The well can have a deeper ratio if the soil around it is very cohesive. However, if the soil is not cohesive, it may need reinforcement. Dug wells have definite depth limitations, for safety and practical reasons, so if your water table is very deep, a dug well may not be the right choice. However, the deeper a well is, the better the quality of the water. This is because water from the surface travels a great distance through the soil and is thus safer, and also because a deeper well will have a larger and more reliable flow, even if the water table drops.

To create a well, mark a circle of ground with a diameter of 4 feet (1.2 meters) or larger at an appropriate location; then, begin digging. After you've dug down about 3 feet (1 meter), place a tripod or log over the well opening to serve as a stabilizing anchor. This anchor can be used with a rope and bucket to remove soil from the bottom of the well as you continue digging.

Ideally, a well should reach about 6.5 feet (2 meters)

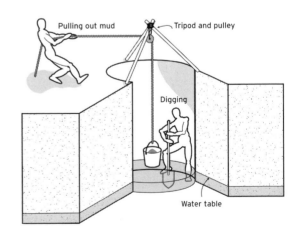

FIGURE 2a: HAND-DIGGING A WELL

below the top of the water table. Stop when the well has reached that depth, or when it's not safe to dig any deeper. The fact that it can be very difficult to determine a safe depth is another reason to look at options other than dug wells. If possible, use sections of culvert or concrete rings to reinforce the walls as you dig, to prevent collapse. Let such supports slide down the walls as you dig deeper.

When you're finished digging, place a layer of gravel at the bottom of the well, if at all possible. This will prevent the well from becoming obstructed by silt. It is generally recommended that you disinfect a well before using it, or after possible contamination. This can be done with a chlorine solution made from bleach. To do so, wash the walls of the well with a 1:50 solution of house-hold bleach and water, but do not use more than 3.2 quarts (3 liters) of bleach.

WELL SAFETY

Wells can be improved for safety, sanitation, and longevity. Here are some ways to protect a well and those who use it:

- Place a cover on the well so that people and debris cannot fall in.

- Always use a clean bucket to draw water from the well.

- If possible, line the walls of the well so that they will not cave in or shed soil into the water over time. You can use bricks and mortar, concrete rings, or whatever sturdy, nontoxic materials you have available.

- To make it easier to raise water from the well, install a hand-pump or a windlass (a hoisting device, commonly made with a rope that winds around a horizontal drum).

- To keep puddles of water from forming around the well (which can create mud and breed mosquitoes), install a stone apron, which will drain water away from the well.

- Secure the well to ensure that people do not enter it unless it is absolutely necessary to do so. Whenever people physically enter a well, they face two possible dangers: the well could collapse on them, or they could contaminate the well.

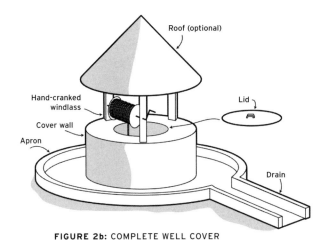

FIGURE 2b: COMPLETE WELL COVER

For additional information, Lifewater Canada has a 100-page manual on wells available online at http://www.lifewater.ca/Section_Tutorial.htm, as well as other information on water. *Waterhole: How to Dig Your Own Well,* by Bob Mellin (Balboa Press, 1992) covers drilling a well with a hand-auger. *Wells and Septic Systems,* by Max and Charlotte Alth (McGraw-Hill Professional, 1991) provides helpful information and tips on how to build your own well or septic system.

ABOUT SPRINGS

Springs are generally an excellent source of clean water. However, in some situations water from a contaminated surface source can travel a short distance in an underground channel and only appear to be a spring. You may want to verify the source.

Springs appear in areas where the water table reaches the surface, generally on the side of a hill or slope. The water is forced out to the surface. Check maps of your area for known spring sites. Also, spring-fed streams may be fuller in the dry season than rain-fed streams. If you can identify spring-fed streams, you can follow them back to the source.

Development and refugee agency handbooks generally recommend "improving" springs to prevent contamination. This may or may not be suitable for your needs, depending on the population density of your area, the nature of the pathogens present, and other factors.

This "improvement" usually entails encasing the spring itself within a container (usually concrete) to prevent direct access by humans or other animals. The water comes from a spout, which is installed on the container. Thus, pathogens cannot be deposited into the spring itself, where they might breed. However, there are some less-invasive methods described in *WELL Technical Brief #34: Protecting Springs: An Alternative to Spring Boxes* (www.lboro.ac.uk/well/resources/technical-briefs/technical-briefs.htm).

RAINWATER IS ANOTHER EXCELLENT SOURCE of clean water, since it is generally free of contamination. However, the supply can vary widely according to climate. Assuming that the roof's surface, gutters, and collection containers are all clean, rainwater can be used safely without treatment.

Since rainwater is such a great source, try to collect as much of it as possible. After a long dry spell, allow the first runoff to flow away to clear dust and such from the roof or catchment. According to the United Nations Environment Programme (UNEP), the ideal roofing for a water source is smooth, dense, and nontoxic. Roof materials they recommend include "corrugated aluminum and galvanized iron, concrete, asphalt or fiberglass shingles, tiles with a neoprene-based coating, and mud." When rainwater will be used for drinking, they suggest avoiding the use of "natural" materials such as thatch, because such roofs may attract insects and rodents and yield contaminated and discolored water. They also suggest that flat ground surfaces, such as runways, can be used for rainwater collection, as long as they are fenced off to prevent access and contamination from humans and animals.

On average, each inch of rainfall will yield about 6.4 gallons per square yard of catchment area. (One millimeter of rainfall will provide about 0.8 liters of water per square meter.) Loss occurs due to evaporation, and varies by climate. In cooler climates you will get closer to 8 gallons per square yard (a full liter per square meter).

There are several types of rainwater catchments. A barrel system includes numerous collection barrels that are connected by pipes; water flows over the

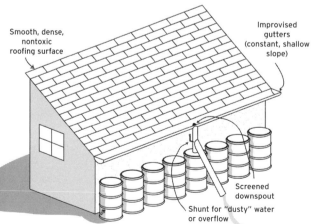

FIGURE 3a: RAINWATER CATCHMENT WITH BARRELS

Smooth, dense, nontoxic roofing surface

Improvised gutters (constant, shallow slope)

Screened downspout

Shunt for "dusty" water or overflow

FIGURE 3b: CATCHMENT BARRELS

roof into a gutter, and then into a centralized downspout. This is an excellent system if you have access to multiple barrel-sized containers, but the fact that there are many holes and piping connections means that there is more potential for leakage and a greater need for maintenance. A single-tank system may be harder to build initially, but it is more reliable and easier to maintain in the long run.

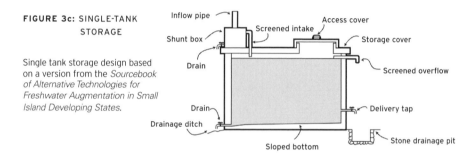

FIGURE 3c: SINGLE-TANK STORAGE

Single tank storage design based on a version from the *Sourcebook of Alternative Technologies for Freshwater Augmentation in Small Island Developing States.*

Water-storage containers should always be covered to prevent contamination. Also, pipes or openings to the tanks (except the faucet) should always be screened to prevent the access and breeding of mosquitoes or other insects.

Snow can also be used as a source of water, but it should be gathered from clean sources away from animal and human traffic to avoid possible contamination. Remember that snow is only as safe as the water it comes from, so treat it if you have any doubts.

Ten portions of snow will yield about one portion of water. If you are melting snow in a container on a fire for drinking, keep topping up the container so that the water doesn't boil and evaporate (unless you believe the water is suspect and should be boiled). Don't try to melt snow in your mouth. In cold climates, this will rob your body of too much valuable heat. If you drink icy cold water, just sip it slowly to limit the effect on your body heat.

For more information on rainwater collection, consult *UNEP, Sourcebook of Alternative Technologies for Freshwater Augmentation in Small Island Developing States* (http://www.unep.or.jp/ietc/Publications/TechPublications/ TechPub-8d/).

SURFACE WATER CAN BE A good source of water, but in many cases it has become contaminated from various sources. Although surface water is easily accessible in many places, it generally requires some sort of treatment.

Sources of surface water include ponds, rivers, and streams. Lively, bubbling streams or rivers with rapids and white water are great sources of drinkable water. The aeration that occurs in flowing water kills most pathogens within a distance of about 33 feet (10 meters), although such water isn't necessarily safe to drink without treatment.

When collecting water from surface sources, try to check for possible sources of pollution. Contamination can come from agricultural and industrial chemicals, soil erosion (especially in areas with industrial farming and logging), garbage, feces from humans and animals, from humans or animals entering or washing in the water and tracking in contaminants or pathogens, or from dead animals in or near the water.

It can be difficult to tell for certain if contamination is present. You may find signs, like dead animals or sewage in the water, which indicate it is definitely not safe to drink. However, there are no signs that prove it is safe to drink. Sources of contamination may come from pipes that enter bodies of water beneath the surface, from garbage or chemical waste that has been buried near the water, or from the groundwater or streams that feed the water in question. Without complex equipment you can't tell for certain if the water is safe, so it is best to assume that it has been contaminated.

Development and refugee agency handbooks offer various suggestions on how to prevent the contamination of surface water. These include fencing ponds and rivers to keep farm animals out, and to discourage people from entering or swimming in sources of drinking water. Generally, they recommend keeping sources of drinking water separate from water used for swimming and washing. To prevent the need to enter a body of water, they suggest building ramps or platforms into the water. This will also reduce erosion.

For more information on protecting a pond as a source of drinking water, see *WELL Technical Brief #47: Improving Pond Water* (www.lboro.ac.uk/well/resources/technical-briefs/technical-briefs.htm).

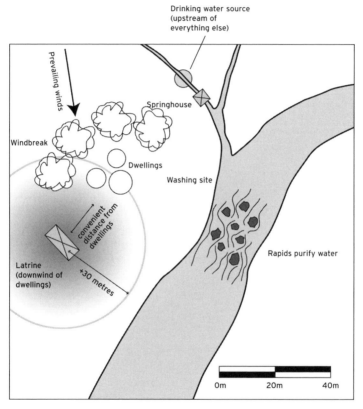

Drinking water source
(upstream of
everything else)

Prevailing winds

Springhouse

Windbreak

Dwellings

Washing site

convenient
distance from
dwellings

+30 metres

Rapids purify water

Latrine
(downwind of
dwellings)

0m   20m   40m

FIGURE 4: WATER MAP

SURVIVAL SOURCES OF WATER ARE ones that are present in small quantities and often are "embodied" in soil or plants. Although we tend to look for water in places such as lakes and streams, it is also possible to extract small quantities of water where it is not visible. These sources are not generally suitable for a large, concentrated population. There are some simple methods for obtaining water from these less-obvious sources.

DUG STILLS

One of the simplest ways to obtain water in a dry area is to dig a hole and place a container in the middle. Then place a clear plastic sheet over the hole with a weight, such as a stone, in the middle and additional weighting along the edges of the hole. The water that evaporates out of the soil will condense and drip into the container. You can also use a flexible hose to suck water out of the container. To provide more water for evaporation, consider adding succulent leaves or vegetable matter to the hole.

The best spots to dig holes for a still include topographical depressions or valleys, areas with green plants, or areas that look damp. However, you should also try to place the still in a sunny location, to encourage more evaporation and condensation.

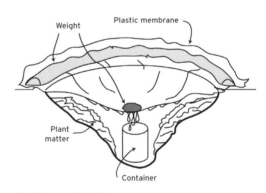

FIGURE 5: DUG STILL

TRANSPIRATION

Trees and other plants naturally release water through their leaves as they breathe. A simple way to capture that water is to place a transparent bag over a branch of a tree or shrub and seal it tightly. Water will condense and collect at the corner of the bag. You can make a small hole or slit to drain the water, and then tie or seal it shut again. Don't bag the branch for too long in hot weather, or it may die. Also, make sure that plants used for transpiration are not poisonous.

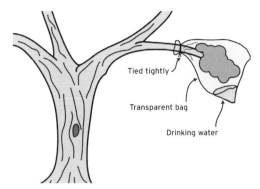

FIGURE 6: COLLECTION WATER FROM TRANSPIRATION

Relatively few plants are actually poisonous. For example, in my region I could use this technique with maples, birches, or hickories. However, I would not use American yew, horse chestnut, or poison sumac, since they have poisonous leaves. I highly recommend investing in one or more thorough plant references, especially ones that relate to your region. Getting to know local flora—especially edible, medicinal, and poisonous plants—can be fun as well as very beneficial.

DEW AND CONDENSATION

In cold, sheltered spots or in the early morning in many locations, you may be able to find dew or condensation on rocks, metal, and vegetation. Use an absorbent cloth as a sponge to collect this water, and then wring it into a container. For example, you can tie cloth around your ankles and walk around in dew-covered grass before sunrise.

WATER IN PLANTS

Bamboo, banana, and plantain trees, palms, and many other plants contain water in their stems that can be accessed by cutting them. To find out whether a plant might offer suitable survival water, consult local sources of knowledge or plant references. Avoid killing a tree for this purpose except in survival situations.

OBSERVING ANIMALS

Watch the behavior of creatures like flies, mosquitoes, bees, doves, and pigeons. They need to travel to find water regularly to survive, and you may be able to follow them to a source.

References on Survival Sources of Water
- *Tom Brown's Field Guide to Wilderness Survival*, Tom Brown Jr. (Berkley Publishing Group, 1983)
- *U.S. Army Survival Manual: FM 21-76 U.S.* (Department of Defense, 1992; available online at http://www.equipped.com/fm21-76.htm)

PART 2

Water Treatment

| SIMPLE TREATMENTS

IF YOU ARE IN DOUBT, treat any water you intend to drink. You can die a lot faster, or be sick for a lot longer, from drinking a drop of contaminated water than you can by drinking no water at all, at least for a limited period of time. The most suitable methods for water treatment will vary based on the circumstances.

Chart 1 compares the effectiveness of various treatment methods in removing contaminants.

CHART 1: EFFECTIVENESS OF WATER TREATMENT METHODS

METHOD	SALTS	PATHOGENS	ODOR & TASTE	TURBIDITY
STRAINING	X	X	X	~
AERATION	X	X	~	X
STORAGE	X	~	~	~
BOILING	X	+	X	X
CHLORINE	X	+	X	X
SOLAR DISINFECTION	X	+	X	X
DISTILLATION	+	+	+	+
SLOW SAND FILTER	X	+	+	+
RAPID SAND FILTER	X	X	~	+

Key: ☐ X ☐ ineffective ☐ ~ ☐ somewhat effective ☐ + ☐ very effective

For a more detailed comparison, see *WELL Technical Brief #48*

STRAINING

Straining turbid (or cloudy) water through a clean handkerchief or other fine, cotton cloth is an effective way to screen larger particles of suspended contaminants such as dirt. It can also remove certain tiny organisms, such as copepods (very small water-dwelling crustaceans), which may carry pathogens. Such organisms are not present in all climates. Straining turbid water will improve the effectiveness of most other treatment methods, and is a good first step.

FIGURE 7: WATER STRAINING

AERATION

Aeration adds air to water and reduces the concentration of volatile substances, such as hydrogen sulfide, that affect the taste and smell of water. It can also oxidize and immobilize elements like iron and manganese that can cause taste and smell problems in water when they are present in excess. (Excessive amounts of iron and manganese in water used for laundering can also stain clothes.)

To aerate water, vigorously shake a partly filled container of water. Another way to aerate water is to pour it through a perforated tray containing small, clean pebbles.

STORAGE

Simply storing untreated surface water will improve its quality. Particles settle to the bottom, and parasites that may be present will die, usually within a few days, without access to a host. Storing water for just twenty-four hours will kill about half of the bacteria that are present. The improvement in quality will be greater at higher temperatures and over longer periods. If you leave cloudy water to settle, remember to take your water from the top layer, once the visible particles have settled. Water containers should always be covered to prevent contamination.

The WELL Resource Centre for Water Sanitation and Environmental Health suggests using a three-container system. Use the first container for newly collected water. If you strain your water, do so as it is poured into this container. After one day, pour water from the first container into the second, being careful to leave sediment or cloudy layers behind to be discarded. Using a tube to siphon water into the second container can help to leave the sediment undisturbed. The next day, pour water from the second container into the third. Water in the third container, which has been stored for at least two days, can then be used for drinking. WELL suggests occasionally rinsing this third container with scalding water to sterilize it.

Glass containers are good for maintaining water quality, but they are heavy and can break. Water can also be stored in food-grade plastic containers. The preferred types of plastic for food are polyethylene terephthalate (PETE), or high-density polyethylene (HDPE). Look for the letters PETE or HDPE or the recycling numbers "1" or "2" stamped on a container's bottom. However, when reusing containers, keep in mind that some chemical substances originally stored in a container may later leach into drinking water that is stored inside that container. For example, a container that held a diet soft drink may later leach the sweetener aspartame into water stored in that container. I recommend not reusing such containers for drinking water. Also, never reuse a plastic container that has stored toxic chemicals.

| # DISINFECTING WATER

DISINFECTION KILLS PATHOGENS IN WATER. It is most effective in water that is relatively free of sediment and organic materials, so it should be the final stage in water treatment, after other contaminants have been removed.

DISINFECTION BY BOILING

Boiling water is a simple and effective method for killing pathogens. At sea level, simply bringing water to a boil will make it safe for drinking. Add one minute to the boiling time for every additional 3,300 feet (1,000 meters) in altitude. According to recommendations by the United Nations, it's not necessary to boil water for five or ten minutes in order for it to be safe. This just wastes fuel. However, the U.S. Centers for Disease Control still advises boiling water for several minutes, due to what they consider a lack of adequate data about how much boiling time is actually required to kill the pathogen that causes hepatitis A.

Be sure to first strain out any large particles through a cloth. If water tastes "flat," pour it back and forth between two containers a few times to aerate it. To improve the taste, as you boil water you can also add a chunk of charcoal from your fire, or some pine needles, removing these before drinking. (When using pine needles, it's important to ensure that they are actually from a pine or other nonpoisonous evergreen, and not a poisonous one like the American yew. Again, a good plant identification guide is extremely useful.)

For more information on boiling water as a disinfection method, see DeWolfe Miller's article, "Boiling Drinking Water; A Critical Look," published in *Waterlines*, Vol. 5, No. 1 (IT Publications, London, 1986). An index to *Waterlines* is available at http://www.itdgpublishing.org.uk/content/WLINdex1to20.htm.

CHEMICAL DISINFECTION

Disinfection by adding chlorine, usually in the form of bleach, is also an option. However, this method is less than ideal. While chlorine is a very effective disinfectant, it can be difficult to determine the proper amount of chlorine to use, and there are potential taste and health side effects that can occur from ingesting chlorine.

The strength of chlorine compounds varies widely and depends on storage conditions. Household bleach rapidly loses its strength over time, though powdered chlorine (calcium hypochlorite) will last longer—up to ten years under ideal storage conditions. Use only pure bleach. Do not use bleach with fabric softener, or other laundry additives, because they are very likely poisonous.

To disinfect clear water with liquid bleach, first look at the concentration of chlorine in your bleach. Then use the following amounts of bleach per quart or liter of water:

1 percent concentration	10 drops
2 to 6 percent	2 drops
7 to 10 percent	1 drop

For slightly cloudy water, use at least double the number of drops. Let the water sit for at least thirty minutes, after which there should be a slight smell of chlorine. If there is no odor, repeat the dose and wait another fifteen minutes. Then let the water sit to reduce the chlorine taste and smell, which may take several hours.

Aerating chlorinated water after disinfection will also improve the taste, as will adding a pinch of powdered vitamin C (crushed vitamin C tablets work), which neutralizes chlorine.

You can also use household, medical iodine to purify water. For 2 percent USP strength, add 5 drops to clear water and 10 drops to cloudy water.

For more information about chemical disinfection, see "Be Prepared with a 3-Day Emergency Food Supply," by E. Schafer, C. Hans, E. Jones Beavers, and D. Nelson (Iowa State University Cooperative Extension, November 1997).

SOLAR DISINFECTION

Solar disinfection works by a combination of exposing water to the sun's ultraviolet (UV) rays and by raising the water's temperature, which kills microorganisms. This technique is most effective in areas that receive large amounts of solar radiation each year (between approximately 35°N and 35°S). For example, the American Southwest and the state of Florida both receive intense solar radiation.

For this method, containers of water are placed in direct sunlight for at least six hours. The water must be relatively clear, and contained within a shallow depth, to allow penetration of UV rays. Placing bottles sideways will increase the solar exposure.

You can use glass containers (except window glass, which does not transmit UV radiation very well), but they are heavier, can break, and take longer to heat up. Plastic bottles made of PETE (polyethylene terephthalate) or

PVC (polyvinyl chloride) are both good choices. However, PETE bottles are preferable, since they are not likely to leach harmful additives into water. (Bottles made of PVC often have a bluish tinge; when burned, they produce a strong and unpleasant smell. PETE burns more easily and has a sweetish smell.) Plastic bottles should be replaced when they start to become scratched and opaque. Newer bottles transmit UV light better. Clear plastic bags of water can also be used quite effectively, since they can store water more shallowly. Plastic bags made out of PETE are again preferable, but they can be difficult to identify, so you may have to rely on whatever food-safe plastic is available. Try to use plastic that has already been used to store food.

The Swiss organization, SANDEC, recommends leaving water out for at least six hours on sunny or partly cloudy days, or for two consecutive days in cloudy weather. This primarily applies to very sunny regions; solar disinfection is not a reliable method in less-sunny regions.

To significantly increase this method's effectiveness, aerate the water by filling the bottle three-quarters full and shaking it for twenty seconds before placing it in the sun. Painting bottles black on one side was originally recommended, but this is no longer recommended because it does not help as much as thought and can actually slow the process on cloudy days. In the middle latitudes, between 35°N and 35°S, solarized water is deemed safe if it reaches a temperature of more than 122° F (50° C) for at least one hour. Putting bottles on corrugated metal roofing will keep them in place and help to increase the temperature. Using reflectors to concentrate sunlight on the water vessel

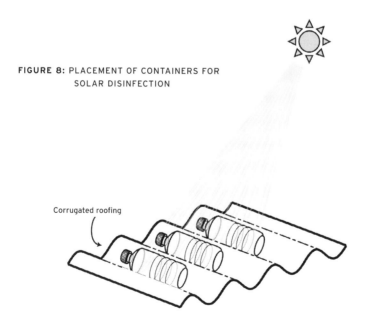

FIGURE 8: PLACEMENT OF CONTAINERS FOR
SOLAR DISINFECTION

Corrugated roofing

will improve effectiveness by increasing the concentration of UV radiation and raising the water's temperature.

Swiss agencies provide extensive information about solar water disinfection at www.sodis.ch.

DISTILLATION

Disinfection by distillation works by evaporating water from a suspect source, which then condenses, leaving distilled water. This is an excellent way to process seawater to create drinking water. Distillation is the only method for removing salt from water that is described in this book.

Water is distilled by using a still, and a stovetop still is quite easy to improvise. It will require the following materials:

a string or a wide, sturdy rubber band
a small plastic sheet
a cup or glass
two small rocks or weights
a heatproof container that can be balanced on top
   of your cooking pot

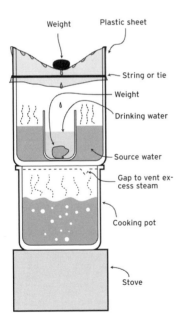

FIGURE 9: STOVETOP STILL

Based on version from RYAN Foundation Handout #655.

To make the still, pour your source water into the heatproof container to a depth of an inch or two. Place one weight in the empty cup, and then put the cup in the middle of the larger container. Then place the plastic sheet on top of the container and secure it (with some extra material in the middle) by wrapping the string or rubber band around it. Put the last weight on top of the plastic sheet so that condensation will run toward the middle and drip into your cup. Then place the completed still on top of a pot that is cooking (assuming that you aren't using a fuel-saving haybox, as discussed in chapter 18).

Solar stills can also be made easily and cheaply to provide a quick source of clean water. They use solar radiation to evaporate water from a contaminated or questionable water source. A solar still can provide enough water for personal use, but not for gardening, since it would need to be as large as the garden itself to yield sufficient water.

To build a solar still, make a small greenhouse from whatever materials you have available. A *cloche-style still* uses windows or plastic to form a framework. Plastic sheeting can also be used, but some people report that water droplets usually do not cling to plastic as well as they do to glass, so they may drop back into the source container. However, the "clinginess" can be improved by lightly rubbing sandpaper over the interior surface of the plastic. If you do use plastic, make sure it is pulled tightly over the frame to avoid flapping or tearing caused by wind.

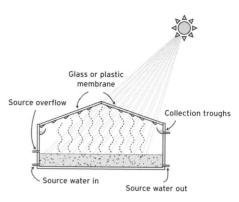

FIGURE 10a: CLOCHE-STYLE SOLAR STILL

You will need to build a basic frame (most simply of wood) to fit the window glass or plastic you have available. The sides of the still can be either glass, plastic, or wooden, depending on what is available. Making them out of a transparent material may increase your yield slightly, but using plywood or similar materials will make it easier to attach your various fittings. All of the parts should be as tight-fitting as possible to avoid the loss of air and moisture.

The source water will go into the bottom of the still. If you have a suitably sized waterproof container (or containers) that are black or dark-colored, you can place those in the bottom of the still structure to fill with water. You can also line the entire bottom of the still with plastic to make it into a large waterproof container. Either the plastic or the material under it will need to be black so that the water will heat up and evaporate from sunlight. Again, if you use plastic, make sure it is a food-grade type, and never use plastic that has come into contact with pesticides, cleaning chemicals, or other poisonous substances. If you plan to place the still on the ground, you may want to insulate beneath the source container.

If you have a slow-trickling supply of water, you can fit a pipe to trickle into the source. Otherwise, you will have to fill it with buckets. Salts and other substances left behind by evaporation will build up in the source water if it is not changed. This means that you will have to remove water with concentrated salts from the still and replace it with new water (albeit infrequently). Simply topping it off will not keep the still running as efficiently as possible.

If you have a continuous trickle of water going into the still, you will want to have a "source-overflow" tube or opening. This prevents incoming water from causing the source-water level from rising up and contaminating the drinking water and can also drain out older source water. The source-overflow tube is simply an opening that allows water to escape, but is screened or small enough to prevent the entry of insects. If you top up your still using containers instead of a continuous trickle, this overflow tube is not necessary.

To collect the drinking water as it drips down the glass or plastic, place a shallow trough, like a large plastic water pipe cut lengthwise, along the lower edge to capture the condensed droplets as they slide down the glass. It will need to be in direct contact with the side of the still in order to prevent water from leaking past it. Place a tube through the side of the still for the trough to drain into a container, where it can be stored until you retrieve it for drinking. If you are using a plastic covering, the easiest way to make the trough may be to cut the plastic larger than it needs to be, and then turn the excess plastic up to form the trough.

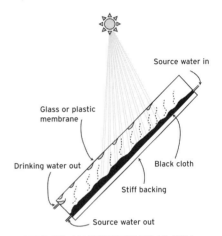

FIGURE 10b: LIGHTWEIGHT SOLAR STILL

You can also make a lightweight, portable solar still based on a design from the excellent resource, *Survival Scrapbook, Volume Two:* by Stefan Szczelkun (1972). Here, a single sheet of plastic on the bottom of the still has two long, narrow troughs at either side for drinking water, and one large trough in the middle for source water. Although this still is much easier to make, you run the risk of source water splashing, slopping, or overflowing into the drinking water supply. This design would also work well on a rooftop.

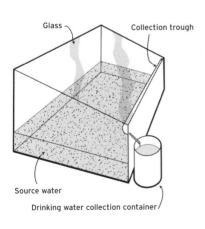

FIGURE 11: ANGLED WINDOW SOLAR SILL

You can also make a solar still using a sloped glass covering. This still functions in much the same way as the cloche-style solar still (Figure 10a), but only requires one large sheet of plastic or glass. The four sides and bottom of the still are wood and lined with plastic, as described above. The glass or plastic is placed on top, and the collective trough is made in the same fashion as above.

To determine the best angle for the glass, see page 68. This same device can be used as a solar food dehydrator, or as a cold frame for gardening. (This is an example of how you can create equipment appropriate to your bioregion and climate. For example, if you have rainy springs, hot, dry summers, and moderate autumns, you can use this device to start your vegetables in the spring, while you are drinking rainwater, and then use it as a still to provide drinking water in the summer, and then to dry garden produce in the fall.) You can make this kind of solar still (dehydrator / cold frame) with 3x6-foot glass patio doors, which are regularly replaced at many apartment buildings. You may be able to buy used glass doors cheaply in bulk. Admittedly, you might not be able to use them all yourself, but your neighbors will thank you when you offer to share. (If you store large quantities of glass, be sure to use spacers between the panes so that they don't touch. If water gets trapped between the panes, it will etch and mar the glass permanently.)

A still can produce about 3.5 quarts per square yard (4 liters of water per square meter) per day, on a good day. You use this approximate figure to match the size of your drinking-water container to the size of your still. The upside of a solar still is that you can even pour wash water into the still to yield drinking water. When using stills, keep in mind that distilled water contains no trace minerals, so it is not ideal as the sole drinking-water source for young children over an extended period of time.

Here's an exercise you might want to try, to practice relying on a still. Build a solar still for you and your family or housemates. What percentage of your water needs can you meet with the water you distill? Can you live for a week on what is produced?

| WATER FILTERS

THE WATER-TREATMENT METHODS DISCUSSED in previous chapters are "batch" methods, rather than continuous ones, which means that they can be labor-intensive. They may also require fuel or chemicals for each use. In contrast, some water filters can operate continuously and don't require materials or labor beyond their initial construction and routine maintenance. This means that they can also produce much larger amounts of clean water and can be made out of available materials, such as barrels and sand.

SLOW SAND FILTERS

In slow sand filtration, the source water flows slowly through a bed of fine sand. The water must be relatively clear and the flow fairly constant for this method to work. Water flows through the filter at a rate of about 4 to 8 inches (10 to 20 centimeters) per hour. The sand depth must be at least 25.6 inches (65 centimeters). The slow sand filter works because of a biologically active microbial film, known as the *schmutzdecke*, which forms on the top layer of the sand and captures and "eats" organisms in the water. The schmutzdecke takes about one to two weeks to form, so water flowing through the filter before that should not be used for drinking. You need to keep water above sand level at all times to keep the schmutzdecke alive. To get a quantity of fine, uniform sand, try sifting available sand through a mosquito net or other fine screen.

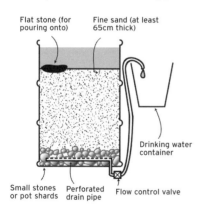

Flat stone (for pouring onto)   Fine sand (at least 65cm thick)

Drinking water container

Small stones or pot shards   Perforated drain pipe   Flow control valve

FIGURE 12a: SLOW SAND FILTER

To assemble the filter, place a perforated drainpipe (with the end covered) into the bottom of the barrel. You will need a hole in the side of the barrel as an exit for the pipe. (You can use caulking to seal around the pipe, but if available, marine epoxy is especially effective.) On the very bottom of the barrel, place a layer of small stones or ceramic pot shards, which will help the water to percolate out the drainpipe more quickly. Then pour in the sand. On the very top, place a flat stone, onto which you will pour your source water. This stone will prevent the flow of water from gouging a hole in the schmutzdecke. You may wish to put a control valve or spigot on the drain-pipe to control the water flow. Alternately, you could attach a flexible hose and lift the end up above water level when you do not want water to flow out.

The filter should be filled with water from the bottom up, to prevent the formation of air bubbles in the sand that would slow the flow of water. This means that initially you will have to fill the filter using the hole that will become the output. To do this, attach a hose or flexible pipe to the spigot that you can elevate above the top of the filter. Using a funnel, or a pressurized or gravity-fed supply of water if available, pour in water until the level reaches the top of the barrel.

Eventually the sand filter will need to be cleaned, because the schmutzdecke will thicken and excessively slow the flow of water. Fortunately, this thickening will not impair the safety of the filter. To clean, drain the water to a level slightly below the top of the sand, and scrape off the very top layer. Then refill it with water from the bottom up. It will require another one or two weeks for the schmutzdecke to regrow.

Remember to always use food-grade containers, and not containers that have been used to store poisonous chemicals. Large, plastic barrels, such as ones used to import pickles for restaurants, are a good option.

RAPID SAND FILTERS

Rapid sand filters work to remove particles and turbidity in water, but do not form a schmutzdecke. They do not kill pathogens.

One type of rapid sand filter is similar to the slow sand filter. However, the water travels upward instead of downward and can move at a faster rate—about 20 inches to 60 inches (.5 to 1.5 meters) per hour. Inside a clean barrel, place a layer of stones at least 6 inches (15 cm) thick, topped by a perforated metal plate, with a thick layer of sand on top of the plate. The sand in this filter must be at least 12 inches (30 cm) thick. Water is added through a pipe at the bottom edge of the barrel, as shown. If you fill it in batches you can use an elevated tube and funnel as discussed above.

A rapid sand filter must be "backwashed" (flushed of sediment by letting the water flow in the opposite direction) regularly, perhaps as often as every day depending on water turbidity and the amount of spare water available for flushing. This is done by pouring sand into the top of the barrel.

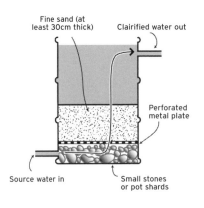

Fine sand (at least 30cm thick)   Clairified water out

Perforated metal plate

Source water in   Small stones or pot shards

FIGURE 12b: RAPID SAND FILTER

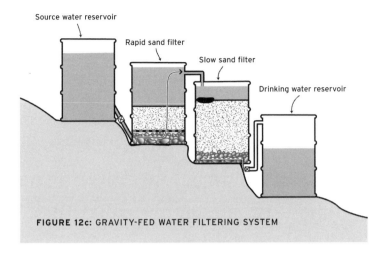

FIGURE 12c: GRAVITY-FED WATER FILTERING SYSTEM

Since slow sand filtration requires clear water, and rapid sand filtration provides clear water, you can put them in a gravity-fed sequence. Additionally, since the maintenance downtime for the slow sand filter is so long, you may want to have several slow sand filters running simultaneously, so that at least one will always be working.

OTHER WATER TREATMENT METHODS

There are a few methods that I did not include in this section, because they didn't fit into the requirements outlined in the Introduction.

Solar pasteurization is a water-treatment method distantly related to solar disinfection, but slightly more difficult. Essentially it involves elevating the temperature of water to more than 149° F (65° C) for more than six minutes, using sunlight or other sources. The advantage is that it does not require UV radiation for disinfection and is more appropriate for nonequatorial latitudes. For more information, check out http://solarcooking.org/docs.htm# Water%20Pasteurization.

There are also numerous commercial, small-scale means of water treatment that may not be appropriate for improvised situations. These include halozone tablets and other chemical treatment resources available at pharmacies or camping/outfitting stores.

References on Sand Filters

For more information on sand filters, consult the following online sources:

- http://www.refugeecamp.org/learnmore/water/slow_sand_filter.htm
- http://www.ce.vt.edu/program_areas/environmental/teach/wtprimer/ slowsand/slowsand.html

- http://www.esemag.com/0500/sand.html
- *WELL Technical Brief #59: Household Water Treatment 2* (www.lboro.ac.uk/well/resources/technical-briefs/technical-briefs.htm)

References on Drinking Water

I consulted the following sources for general information about drinking water:

- The IRC International Water and Sanitation Centre has an extensive online database of water-related publications at www.irc.nl/ircdoc/.
- *UNHCR (United Nations High Commissioner for Refugees) Water Manual for Refugee Situations* and *UNHCR Handbook for Emergencies*. These and other UN refugee references are available online at: www.the-ecentre.net/resources/e_library/index.cfm.
- *WELL Technical Briefs,* available at www.lboro.ac.uk/orgs/well/resources/technical-briefs/technical-briefs.htm
- *Water for the World Technical Notes* offers extensive information on water and sanitation (www.lifewater.org/wfw/wfwindex.htm).
- *The Drinking Water Book,* by Colin Ingram (Ten Speed Press, 1991)

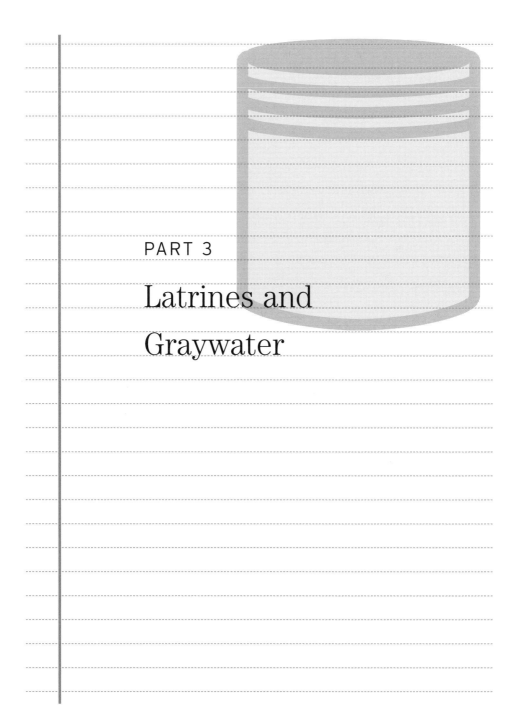

PART 3

Latrines and Graywater

CHAPTER 9

LATRINES

IN THE EVENT OF AN infrastructure failure, dealing with solid waste becomes an important priority. Feces contain and potentially transmit a variety of pathogens, including bacteria, viruses, and worms. Exposed feces also attract flies, which may spread diseases.

Latrines are structures that collect solid waste in one place, prevent access by insects, keep water from being contaminated, offer some privacy to the users, and in some cases, provide usable fertilizer.

HOW TO SITE LATRINES

Due to potential groundwater contamination, latrines should be at the very least 100 feet (30 meters) from any well, body of water, or potential drinking-water source (though this is less of a problem with most composting toilets). Doctors Without Borders/Médicins Sans Frontières (the international humanitarian organization) recommends a distance of at least 165 feet (50 meters) from water. Latrines should also be a reasonable distance from dwellings—no less than about 16.5 feet (5 meters) because of possible smell problems, but no more than about 165 feet (50 meters) for convenience. They should also be downwind of dwellings, especially the improvised types. For hygienic purposes, there should be a source of soap and wash water near all latrines.

Choose a site that is not likely to flood. When digging a pit, leave at least 5 feet (1.5 meters) between the bottom of the pit and the top of the water table. The depth of the water table can be difficult to determine, but you can try to estimate it by determining the depth of nearby wells or ponds, by obtaining water table data from your area, or by digging or drilling a smaller test hole.

PIT LATRINES

The simplest type of latrine is a pit with some form of covering. In a wilderness setting, with only a few people, feces can simply be buried shallowly in the soil, at least 100 feet (30 meters) from water. Organisms in the soil will efficiently break down the solid waste.

In a setting with a denser population, a larger pit is required. Sizing the pit is important. The amount of solid waste that each person produces per day varies widely based on diet and other factors. A good general estimate is to assume that one person will excrete about 1.4 cubic feet (.04 m3) of solids per year. (The water content is less important, since it will drain out or evaporate.) So for 25 people, you will need a pit volume of at least 35 cubic feet (1 m3) per year of use (25 x 0.04 m3 = 1.00 m3).

In calculating the pit volume, include about 20 inches (50 cm) of depth from the surface for adding soil back into the pit. Set aside excavated soil for this purpose.

Build some type of basic structure on top of the pit with the materials that are available. It is important to have a close-fitting cover for the pit to reduce odors and keep out flies. It's also a good idea to place shallow drainage ditches near the latrine to direct rainwater around and away from the latrine. If heavy rain runs into a latrine it can cause the latrine to overflow, thus spreading the contents and any pathogens that are present.

Elevated seats are common in my culture. However, many people find a squatting position more comfortable. There is some evidence that this is healthier, and it is certainly easier to make a simple hole in a board. However, this may be less appropriate for people who have difficulty standing up from a squatting position. If small children are afraid of falling into the hole, you can make a covering for the hole, with a smaller hole within it, or simply make a second, appropriately sized hole in the floor.

If the water table is too high, or the soil is too shallow or tough for digging, you can make the pit within an elevated earth mound and/or use a barrel with a perforated or removed bottom and elevate the structure above it.

Depending on your soil type, and the shape and depth of the pit, you may need to line the pit with rocks or old barrel drums (with the tops and bottoms cut off) to prevent it from collapsing. However, the lining should be porous at the bottom to allow liquids to leave the pit. If smells are a problem, users can put soil, wood ashes, or sawdust into the pit after each use. Wood ash (especially hardwood ash) is effective at limiting both smell and fly problems. After a period of use, when there is only about 20 inches (50 cm) between the surface and contents of the pit, move the latrine structure to a new site and refill the full pit with soil.

TRENCH LATRINES

Extend the basic pit latrine out into a line and you have a trench latrine. It's pretty self-explanatory.

Trenches can be dug in rows to increase density. Zigzagging dividers can be placed for privacy. The trench latrine is generally considered an emergency measure, suitable for high population densities. Both trench and pit latrines should be upgraded as soon as possible to a more hygienic system, such as the next latrine described.

VENTILATED IMPROVED PIT LATRINES

An enhancement of the basic pit latrine, the ventilated improved pit (VIP) latrine is designed to address odor and fly problems (see Figure 13, below). A ventilation pipe is added and extends at least 20 inches (50 cm) above the top of the shelter roof. As air moves across the top of the pipe, it draws air up and out of the shelter and pit. A mosquito net on top of the pipe traps flies inside, where they die. The interior of the shelter should be relatively dim, so that flies are attracted to the light from the pipe. This latrine does not include a lid for

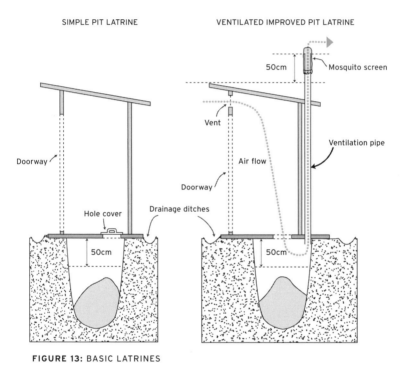

FIGURE 13: BASIC LATRINES

the hole, since air is constantly drawn through, keeping smells to a minimum, but you may need to use a cover anyway in less windy areas.

Pit, trench, and VIP latrines can be constructed quickly and easily. They are all relatively safe, provided that they are not close to a food or water source. Sanitation is aided by the fact that no one has to handle solid or liquid waste; the hole is simply refilled.

However, these types of latrines are likely to introduce pathogens into the groundwater, even if the pathogens are present only near the latrines. Also, the breakdown of feces occurs mostly as an anaerobic ("without air") process that produces a variety of gases, including methane (odorless) and hydrogen sulfide (which smells like rotten eggs).

OTHER OPTIONS

Additional options include the pour-flush latrine. The pour-flush latrine has a U-shaped water seal (the same concept as you might find underneath many indoor sinks) that reduces smells and flies. The liquid effluent drains into a leaching pit.

One result of using the above types of latrines is that the nutrients in solid and liquid wastes are lost in the pit, which means that gardeners must find alternate sources of valuable nutrients like nitrogen. (On an organic farm, a primary source of nitrogen is animal waste.) Many soils have already been mined of nutrients, and they can benefit from the nutrients present in feces. Besides, for many people during industrial collapse, the only source of animal manure for gardening may be their own. The main alternative to the pit toilet is the composting toilet, described in chapter 10.

References on Latrines

For more information on latrines, consult the following:

- *World Health Organization Briefs*
  www.who.int/docstore/water_sanitation_health/onsitesan/ch04.htm
  www.who.int/water_sanitation_health/hygiene/om/en/linkingchap8.pdf
- *WELL Technical Briefs* (www.lboro.ac.uk/orgs/well/resources/
  technical-briefs/technical-briefs.htm)
- *UNHCR (United Nations High Commissioner for Refugees)
  Handbook for Emergencies* and *UNHCR Water Manual for
  Refugee Situations*
  (www.the-ecentre.net/resources/e_library/index.cfm).

| COMPOSTING TOILETS

COMPOSTING IS AN AEROBIC PROCESS–meaning it takes place with the presence of air. That means that properly operating composting toilets do not produce unpleasant smells or gases. The temperatures reached inside the compost, along with the time the compost spends "curing," kill any disease organisms present. Composting toilets also conserve the nutrients in feces and urine, so that they can be returned to the land. Compost itself contains valuable organic matter that does wonders for soil life and gardens.

Some people worry about the fact that one might have to handle material containing human feces. This is a valid concern, but it shouldn't be a problem when appropriate hand washing and other simple precautions take place. As long as you wash properly, a composting toilet is no more dangerous than any other kind of toilet.

For more extensive information on the subject of composting toilets, read the well-written and thoroughly researched *The Humanure Handbook* by Joseph Jenkins. (He uses the term *humanure* to refer to human excrement.) You can visit http://weblife.org/humanure, where the entire text is available online.

HOW COMPOSTING WORKS

Composting is a process by which microorganisms, which are normally present in the soil and all around us, break down organic materials like kitchen scraps, straw, excrement, and so on. Essentially, the organisms eat these materials. As they do so, they also generate heat, just as our bodies generate heat during digestion. When composting occurs in a dense-enough pile, the heat increases to the point where any pathogens are killed. A class of microbes—called thermophilic microorganisms—love high temperatures. If you can get a compost pile up to thermophilic temperatures—above 113° F (45° C)—composting happens very rapidly.

A well-made compost will be quite warm and it will not smell. The essential ingredients of good compost are sufficient moisture, oxygen, a warm-enough temperature, and a good balance between carbon and nitrogen.

The compost should not be too dry, or too wet. If it's too dry, the microorganisms will not be able to grow properly, and valuable nitrogen will be lost to the air. If it's too wet, air won't be able to get in and the compost will become anaerobic (and smelly). A compost should be about as damp as a wrung-out sponge. If your compost is too dry, just add household wastewater. If it is too wet, you need to add more bulky material, such as straw or the other roughage materials discussed below.

Giving a compost pile oxygen means giving it air. This is why bulky materials, known as roughage, are so important. You can use sawdust, dry leaves, leaf mold (decaying leaves), peat moss, weeds, hay, straw, rice hulls, shredded paper or cardboard, or similar materials. If something in the compost pile smells bad, cover it with this bulky material.

Temperature is important because the thermophilic composting microbes need a minimum temperature to operate, and because the elevated temperature kills pathogens. In cold climates, some pathogens will sleep over winter, but the compost pile will come alive again in the spring. (However, freezing does kill some pathogens.)You can continue to add compost to the pile even if it is frozen.

A good carbon-to-nitrogen ratio helps the compost to heat up by giving the microbes a healthy, balanced diet. The bulky materials listed above are very high in carbon. Adding manure and urine as well as grass clippings and vegetable and fruit waste or peelings helps to equalize the nitrogen ratio. A good ratio of carbon to nitrogen is somewhere between 20:1 and 35:1. If there is too much nitrogen in your compost, it will release that nitrogen as ammonia gas, which you don't want. Not only will you lose nitrogen, but it also smells bad.

Many people do not urinate in their composting toilets, because they find that it causes an odor. This smell comes from excess nitrogen and water, and adding roughage materials (as described above) compensates for that. Jenkins recommends including urine in a well-balanced compost, but most people I know who use composting toilets simply apply their urine (diluted with at least 3 to 6 parts of water) to their garden or orchard. Of course, this may be more convenient for men than for women. (Urine is almost universally free of pathogens. Only urinary schistosomiasis can be spread by urine* and it exists only in a few tropical locations.) See what works for you with your climate and soils. If putting urine in your composting toilet isn't working, your nose will tell you quickly. Separating urine may also be a good idea in situations where the nitrogen content is required immediately for gardening, and the gardener cannot wait for the compost to cure.

----

* One recent study found that prions (the biological particles that cause mad cow disease) can be excreted in urine. However, there is currently no evidence that prions persist in the soil intact, or that they could be taken up into plant tissues.

Refer to the references listed at the end of this chapter for comprehensive tables of the carbon and nitrogen contents of different foods and organic materials.

COMPOSTING TOILET OPTIONS

There are many types of commercial composting toilets. In keeping with the focus of this book, I will discuss those that you can make yourself. Two types that are especially suited to the criteria described in the Introduction are the Jenkins sawdust toilet and the two-chamber moldering toilet.

THE JENKINS SAWDUST TOILET

Described by Joseph Jenkins in *The Humanure Handbook,* the sawdust toilet is a convenient method of composting humanure while having a toilet inside your home. This method consists of a toilet receptacle inside a dwelling, which is filled with roughage materials (such as shredded paper or cardboard, sawdust, dry leaves, hay, straw, or rice hulls) and a set of composting bins located outside, into which the toilet receptacle is regularly emptied.

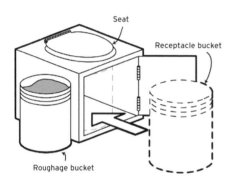

Seat

Receptacle bucket

Roughage bucket

FIGURE 14: COMPOSTING TOILET RECEPTACLE

The inside receptacle is simple to construct and can be made in a several ways. Using a 5-gallon bucket is easy, since it's commonly available. Jenkins does not recommend using a larger receptacle than that, since the contents would be very heavy to carry to the pile. You can build a toilet seat on top of the receptacle, or a platform on which to squat.

After each "deposit," add roughage material to cover the waste. This toilet does not require an airtight or fly-proof lid, since the roughage keeps out flies and cuts odors. When the receptacle is full (or almost too heavy to carry), it can be dumped in the compost bin and buried in the top layer of the compost pile.

There are numerous designs for compost bins, many of which vary by climate. In hot, dry climates, you may need to dig a pit for compost to conserve valuable moisture. In very rainy climates, you may need to build a roof over a compost pile to keep it dry enough and to prevent nutrients from leaching away.

Jenkins suggests a simple rotating multi-bin system. Remember that you will need at least two bins, one for this year's compost pile (still being built), and one for last year's pile that is composting. If climate or other constraints prevent your compost pile from reaching thermophilic temperatures, you

will want to add a third bin to let the compost mature for a full two years. You may
also want an extra, sheltered bin to store
roughage materials such as straw, grass,
or hay.

When starting a new humanure compost pile, create a base of roughage materials at least 18 inches high. This "sponge"
will prevent contamination by soaking up
any fluid that leaches from the pile.

If your compost pile does not produce
any smells, you may not have trouble with
animals digging into the pile. However, if
such invasions pose a concern, prevent animals from accessing the pile and spreading
pathogens by surrounding the pile with wire fencing or some other barrier.

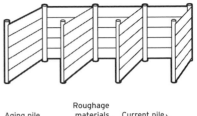

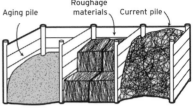

Roughage
Aging pile   materials   Current pile

FIGURE 15: THREE-BIN COMPOST SYSTEM

THE TWO-CHAMBER TOILET

This composting toilet is essentially an outhouse version of the general system described above. The "bathroom" is located
directly above the composting chamber.
There are two seats (or holes, if you prefer
to squat), one for each chamber. After each
deposit, roughage material is dropped into
the chamber. Only one chamber is in use at
any given time; the other one is composting
and closed off.

You can make the chamber out of cement, wood, or other available materials.
However, it need not be airtight or
leakproof. You will need a door on the
"back" to access the compost to check on
it and eventually empty the chamber. You
may need to periodically smooth the pile,
check the moisture, and add more roughage material.

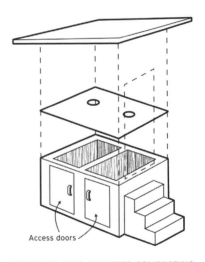

Access doors

FIGURE 16: TWO-CHAMBER COMPOSTING
LATRINE

VARIATIONS

There are plenty of variations on simple and home-built composting toilet designs. To increase the composting temperature, some toilets use solar energy to
heat the pile and accelerate decomposition. You can enhance the two-chamber design by facing the chambers toward the south and placing glass or

translucent plastic on the wall to let in sunlight. You could even include reflectors to heat things up even more.

Some designs also include perforated pipes or other means of increasing the air supply to the compost pile. Others creatively incorporate reused barrels or other materials in their toilets. Check out various designs and experiment for yourself.

References on Composting Toilets and Composting
For more information, consult the following:
- www.compostingtoilet.org
- *The Humanure Handbook: A Guide to Composting Human Manure,* Third Edition, by Joseph C. Jenkins (Jenkins Publishing, 1999)
- *The Toilet Papers: Recycling Waste and Conserving Water,* by Sim Van Der Ryn (Chelsea Green Publishing, 1999)
- *The Real Dirt: The Complete Guide to Backyard, Balcony, and Apartment Composting* by Mark Cullen and Lorraine Johnson (Penguin Books, 1992)

| # USING GRAYWATER

GRAYWATER IS WATER THAT HAS been used in washing dishes, laundry, bathing, and so on. It does not contain nearly as many nutrients as humanure or urine, and it can contain some pathogens. Thus, graywater should be treated with reasonable caution when it is recycled. It can also contain food scraps that might attract rodents and other animals or produce smells. To avoid these problems, it's good to get graywater into the soil as efficiently as possible.

Because graywater can contain pathogens, it should not be applied directly to vegetables growing in the garden. However, it can be applied to fruit trees or bushes, which is an excellent way to reuse the water and any nutrients it contains. (The difference between these types of plants is that vegetables can directly absorb pathogens from their environment into plant tissue that is then eaten. In contrast, fruit trees or bushes draw water up from the roots to the fruit, but the pathogens are kept at ground level and do not travel up the plant stem.) Graywater should not be poured into streams or bodies of water.

Depending on how much graywater you produce, you can pour at least part of it into your compost pile, assuming that this won't make the compost too wet. That is one of the best ways to deal with it.

GRAYWATER PIT

The simplest way to dispose of graywater, and one especially appropriate for camping or wilderness situations, is to dig a pit about 1 foot wide by 2 feet deep (3 meters by .6 meters). Graywater pits should be built a safe distance from water sources like streams and wells, at least 100 feet (30 meters), depending on soil conditions. To create a grease trap and screen for food scraps, place crisscrossed sticks and long grasses over the top. Then regularly burn the sticks and grasses in your fire.

You can build a larger pit as well, such as one made from a drum-style barrel with large holes punched in it, or the bottom cut out. To prevent access by rodents, partially fill the barrel with stones and gravel, so that it will be difficult for animals to dig their way to any food remnants.

In cold climates, you may have trouble with graywater freezing in winter, or snow covering the graywater pit. If possible, site the pit behind a windbreak, so that the prevailing winds will not drift snow over the top of it. The heat from wash water and the heat from the soil should help avert freezing except in extremely cold areas, in which case you will simply have to wait for the water to thaw in spring. The branching system described below is not ideal for very cold climates in winter.

BRANCHING GRAYWATER SYSTEM

The downside of a simple graywater pit is that one area receives a lot of water and nutrients, perhaps too much, while other areas do not get enough. You can improvise a branching system to distribute graywater to a larger area, such as an orchard. This system works using a downhill grade. Water is channeled from the house, washing site, or dump site to mulch-covered troughs.

The channels may be simple, improvised, shallow trenches in the soil's surface, depending on conditions. Better yet, they may be covered, filled in with gravel and small stones, or replaced by pipes. These channels must slope downhill continuously, or the water will back up or pool.

The destinations are shallow depressions or trenches full of mulch. The water may go directly into the mulch, or into a gravel-filled container, which then releases the water into the mulch. Alternately, water could be poured directly into the gravel bucket, as an improved pit system.

References on Graywater
- *Create an Oasis with Graywater: Your Complete Guide to Managing Graywater in the Landscape*, by Art Ludwig. You can visit the author's website at www.oasisdesign.net.
- *The Humanure Handbook: A Guide to Composting Human Manure*, Third Edition, by Joseph C. Jenkins (Jenkins Publishing, 1999)
- *Fieldbook for Canadian Scouting* (Boy Scouts of Canada, 1986)

PART 4

Keeping Food Cool

| # SOME BASICS ABOUT HEAT AND COOLING

WHENEVER WE TALK ABOUT COOKING and cooling, we are referring to the movement of heat and the devices we make to gain, lose, and store heat. Heat storage is the same as thermal mass. A heavy, massive object, such as a steel anvil, a barrel of water, or a brick wall, can absorb and store a lot of heat. It takes a significant heat gain to heat up a large mass and a major heat loss to cool it down. In contrast, air has very little thermal mass and it heats or cools easily. This is also why being in air at 212° F (100° C) is merely uncomfortable, while being in water at 212° F (100° C) is lethal. Much more heat is stored in water than in air, and water conducts that heat into your body more easily.

THE MOVEMENT OF HEAT

Heat moves in one of three ways: through convection, conduction, and radiation. Convection moves heat by a circulation of fluid, conduction through direct contact, and radiation through light and infrared light.

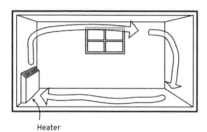

FIGURE 17a: CONVECTION

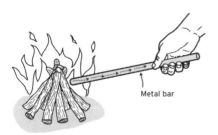

FIGURE 17b: CONDUCTION

Convection is the movement of heat by circulation within a fluid (a gas or liquid). As air over a heater warms and rises, it draws in cool air nearby, which also warms and rises. As this air gradually gives its heat to the ceiling, it sinks down to start again. Many people think that heat rises, but heat itself will go in any direction. Instead, warm fluids, like air, tend to rise. The heat within those fluids is then released into the cooler things that they touch.

Conduction is the direct movement of heat through an object. When you stick a metal rod into a fire, heat moves along the rod by conduction and gradually heats up the other end.

Radiation is the movement of heat directly from a warm body outward. Examples of radiant heat include warmth emanating from sunlight, or heat from a fire. This happens because any warm body emits infrared light (and other invisible forms of energy), thus warming objects by its rays.

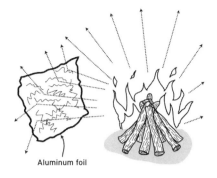

Aluminum foil

FIGURE 17c: RADIATION

Understanding the ways that heat moves is essential to managing heating and cooling devices and systems. When you want to thwart the movement of heat away from the food you are cooking to conserve fuel, or thwart the movement of heat into the food you want to keep cool, consider how heat transfers and how you can slow or hasten its movement.

To slow heat loss by convection, minimize or eliminate air pockets or gaps in which air can circulate. Air will not circulate in gaps less than about 3/8 of an inch (1 cm) across. To slow heat loss by conduction, insulate with a material that has many tiny air pockets, which slow the movement of heat. To slow heat loss by radiation, use a "radiant barrier" like aluminum foil, which reflects heat.

When designing a device for heating or cooling, we want to consider the concepts of heat gain, heat loss, and heat storage. Heat gain just means heat is moving into or being generated in the device; heat loss means heat is moving out of it. For cooking, we want to maximize heat gain and heat storage (within reasonable levels) and minimize heat loss. In cooling food to keep it fresh, we want to maximize heat loss and heat storage, and to minimize heat gain.

| COOLING AND FOOD SAFETY

AS WE ALL KNOW, KEEPING food cool extends its storage life and makes it safer to eat. Ultimately, effective food storage can reduce waste, promote health, and decrease negative impacts on a land base by reducing the amount of land required for farming or gardening.

In keeping things cool, we want to minimize heat gain to our cooling device and maximize heat loss and heat storage. To minimize heat gain, it's best to put a cooler in the coolest place possible. Keep it in the shade to avoid heat gains from sunlight. Also move it away from hot objects; obviously, we would not put an icebox next to a woodstove. Insulation around a cooler stops heat from infiltrating the container to warm the food.

Several techniques maximize heat loss. Evaporation is an excellent way to carry heat away from your cooler, just as sweat carries heat away from your skin to cool you down. Modern refrigerators use a fluid that is evaporated and condensed in pressurized coils, which is a variation on this basic idea. Heat can also be carried away by conduction, such as by a cool stream in which jars of food are placed, or by cool, moist earth underground. Adding ice is another way to get rid of heat. The ice cools the compartment and, as the ice melts, the draining trickle of water carries away the heat.

Maximizing heat storage, within reasonable limits, is important to moderate temperature variations that result from short-term changes in weather, like cool nights and warm days, or when a cooler door is opened to allow heat inside. Cold holes and root cellars use the thermal mass of the earth itself, which absorbs away extra heat. We will look at tools that rely on all these approaches.

FOOD SAFETY

Without standardized industrial refrigeration, it may be difficult to ascertain the safety of various foods. Smell food to check for spoilage, but remember that food that smells fine isn't necessarily safe. Here are some general guidelines to keep in mind.

Fruits and Vegetables

Fresh produce generally does not need to be refrigerated, but should be kept as cool as possible. Apples, pears, avocados, apricots, and some other fruits release a gas (ethylene) that causes ripening, so many fruits and vegetables will keep longer if they are kept separate from these fruits.

Meats
Large, solid pieces of meat from mammals, such as rump roasts, will last the longest. Uncured sausage lacks preservatives and may spoil. Chopped, raw meats (like hamburger) will spoil quickly and should be eaten as soon as possible; even when kept relatively cool, they may spoil in as little time as twelve hours.

Dairy
Hard cheeses will last a long time at room temperature. Soft cheeses, like cream cheese, will spoil more quickly; watch for bad flavor or mold. Unrefrigerated milk spoils quickly; however, sour milk can be used for baking or to make cheeses.

Miscellaneous Foods
Custard, gravies, creamed foods, chopped meats, poultry, and seafood sandwich fillings will spoil very quickly when brought to room temperature. Canned food that has been frozen may still be edible, if it looks and smells good. However, do not taste it! If you do eat food from cans that are suspect, but probably safe, boil the food for at least ten to twenty minutes to avoid botulism. Food from cans that are burst or punctured should not be eaten.

Food Safety References
- "Safety of Refrigerated Foods after a Power Failure," University of Florida Institute of Food and Agricultural Sciences, 1997.

COLD HOLES, COLD CELLARS, AND root cellars all use the coolness of the earth to create cold storage. These proven methods have been used by humans for tens of thousands of years, if not longer.

A cold hole is simply a well-like tunnel dug into the earth. The sides can be secured with old metal barrels, stacked on top of one another with the tops and bottoms removed. Food is put into a crate or bucket and lowered on a rope into the hole, which is kept covered. It can be as shallow as a few feet deep, or ten feet or more, as appropriate. The depth of the water table within a given location will be a factor in how deep to dig a cold hole.

A cold cellar (also called a root cellar) is a room built into the ground, often as part of a house. Although cold cellars can rely solely on the temperature of the earth around them, the cold cellar pictured works with the help of passive convection (much like a cold room, which will be discussed in chapter 16). Warm air rises and is drawn out of the cellar through the upper tube as cold air simultaneously sinks in through the lower tube. This circulation will happen more at night and on colder days. Elevating the warm air "exhaust" pipe higher above ground level will help wind passing across the tube opening to draw out warm air. Larger tube diameters, around 3 inches (5 cm) across, will allow air to circulate more easily. Place screen and/or mesh over the external openings to keep out rodents and insects.

If you are building a cold cellar, one thing to keep in mind is that a forced-air heating system can create a pressure

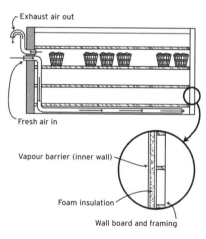

Exhaust air out

Fresh air in

Vapour barrier (inner wall)

Foam insulation

Wall board and framing

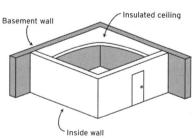

Insulated ceiling

Basement wall

Inside wall

FIGURE 18a: BASEMENT ROOT CELLAR

differential in parts of your house. This is caused by leaks in the existing duct-work, which, unfortunately, can be difficult to locate and fix after the ducts have been installed. If any given room has either less or more pressure than outside, that room could either draw air in or push it out through both air pipes simultaneously, impairing the convection effect. That means that if a cold cellar isn't well sealed from adjacent rooms, and the forced-air system is running, the convection effect may not work as well as it should.

Small-scale, improvised root cellars are easy to make. If you have an old refrigerator, you can remove the electrical connections (and anything else you might want to salvage or keep out of the ground) and bury it, back side down, in the ground. Leave just a few inches and the door above ground. The shelves form ready-made vegetable storage compartments. In climates with very cold winters, pile straw, leaves, or other mulches on top of the "cellar."

Any large container buried in the ground can serve the same function. Try barrels or garbage cans (but never use containers which have stored pesticides or other toxins). Make sure to keep the container away from moisture and puddles, so that water does not seep in and waterlog or freeze the produce, or freeze the container shut. Also ensure that the container has a top that closes tightly enough to keep out rodents. Place a deep layer of leaves or straw on top, for insulation and to keep snow off. You may need to put boards, a tarp, or chicken wire above the insulation to keep it in place.

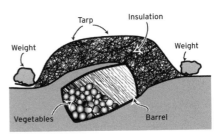

FIGURE 18b: BARREL ROOT CELLAR

You can also take a chest freezer or refrigerator and bury it in the ground up to the lid. First, drain the coolant and compressor pump (which may contain toxic petroleum products that could leak into the soil). I used a buried freezer with straw bales and a tarp on top to keep root vegetables last winter, and it was very effective. The main problem you might encounter is that the lack of ventilation and the moisture given off by the vegetables can cause a buildup of condensation on the walls and lid. You can either wipe off the lid and sides with a cloth when you get a batch of vegetables, or try drilling a small, screened opening in the lid to exchange air. Just make sure that rain or rodents cannot get in through the opening. Also, take precautions to make sure that an old refrigerator or freezer will not pose a safety hazard for children, who may try to crawl inside.

You can also make a wire or metal box on the ground and then stack square bales of hay or straw around it to keep out rodents and to provide insulation. To provide additional insulation, you can also line the box with Styrofoam or other insulating materials.

Separate storage fruits and vegetables from each other and they will last longer because the ethylene produced by some fruits will not induce the vegetables to ripen or sprout. If you cannot store them in separate locations, ensure that you have adequate ventilation to prevent ethylene gas from building up. Many vegetables can be stored in root cellars, including potatoes, carrots, beets, turnips, salsify, and parsnips. Temperature and humidity requirements vary among fruits and vegetables. The sidebar below lists many fruits and vegetables by their needs. An asterisk (*) indicates that they will tolerate only short-term storage. Relative humidity is measured with a simple device called a hygrometer, which is readily available at hardware stores next to the thermometers. Sometimes both instruments are combined. It's a good idea to monitor both temperature and relative humidity and to arrange your storage of produce accordingly.

CHART 2: OPTIMUM STORAGE CONDITIONS FOR FRUITS AND VEGETABLES

COLD AND VERY MOIST

(32–40° F / 0–5° C and 90 to 95 percent relative humidity)

Carrots	Beets	Parsnips
Rutabagas	Turnips	Celery
Chinese Cabbage	Celeriac	Leeks
Salsify*	Winter Radishes	Kohlrabi
Collards*	Broccoli*	Horseradish*
Jerusalem Artichokes		

COLD AND MOIST

(32–40° F / 0–5° C and 80 to 90 percent relative humidity)

Potatoes	Cabbage	Apples
Oranges	Grapefruit	Pears
Grapes* *(40° F / 5° C)*	Cauliflower*	

COOL AND MOIST

(40–50° F / 5–10° C and 85 to 90 percent relative humidity)

Cucumbers*	Cantaloupe
Muskmelon	Sweet Peppers* *(45–55° F / 7–13° C)*
Watermelon	Eggplant* *(50–60° F / 6–10° C)*
Ripe Tomatoes*	

COOL AND DRY

(32–50° F / 0–10° C and 60 to 70 percent relative humidity)

Garlic (keeps best at around 50 percent humidity)

Onions

Green Soybeans (in the pod)*

MODERATELY WARM AND DRY

(50–60° F / 6–10° C and 60 to 70 percent relative humidity)

Dry Hot Peppers	Pumpkins
Sweet Potatoes	Winter Squash
Green Tomatoes	

Root Cellar Reference

An excellent resource about in-ground food storage is *Root Cellaring: Natural Cold Storage of Fruits and Vegetables* by Mike and Nancy Bubel, 2nd Edition (Storey Publishing, 1991).

CHAPTER 15

ICE CAVES, ICE HOUSES
AND ICEBOXES

ICE CAVES AND ICE HOUSES

In climates where a major amount of ice forms in winter, or even where a significant amount of snow falls, this technique might be applicable. Ice caves and ice houses are designed to store ice produced during winter for later use.

In the northern hemisphere, ice caves can be dug into the northern side of hills. Alternatively, a very well-insulated shed or shack can be built to store ice. In either case, insulation, such as straw, is also placed on the ground and between the blocks of ice. You may want to provide some sort of drainage channel for meltwater, depending on your design and climate conditions.

Historically, ice was usually cut from bodies of water and dragged to a storage space. If you don't have access to a body of water that freezes over with enough ice, you can pile up snow and walk on it with snowshoes and boots to tamp it down. Try to compress it as much as possible, and then leave it for a few hours to solidify. Then cut blocks of packed snow and store them as you would store ice. However, the compressed snow blocks will not last as long because they are much less dense (any given volume of snow is about 90 percent air). They also probably won't be as clean as ice blocks.

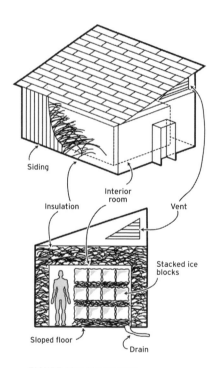

FIGURE 19a: ICE HOUSE

ICEBOXES

An icebox is a simple insulated box or cooler into which ice is placed. This device preceded the refrigerator in the Western world, which is why refrigerators are sometimes called iceboxes.

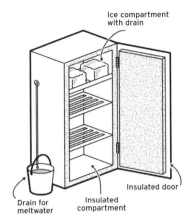

Ice compartment
with drain

Insulated door

Drain for
meltwater

Insulated
compartment

FIGURE 19b: ICEBOX

Ice will last longer if there is a tube to drain water away from the ice as it melts. If possible, place the ice in a tray or compartment at the top of the cooler, since cold air sinks down. Foods that need to be iced or kept very cold are put into that top compartment in direct contact with the ice.

CHAPTER 16

WATER IMMERSION, COLD ROOMS, AND EVAPORATIVE COOLING

IN THIS CHAPTER, WE'LL DISCUSS a variety of alternative cooling systems. Most are simple procedures and require only minimal equipment.

WATER IMMERSION

A *spring house* is a shed or insulated chest built adjacent to or over a spring or small, cold stream. Inside, water flows through a tray, in which are placed containers of food to be kept cold. A similar system could also work at the edge of a cold lake or river: water could be channeled into the tray, or a covered cage could be securely placed within the water. Watertight jars are indispensable in this kind of cooler. Shade will also help keep this type of system cool on sunny days.

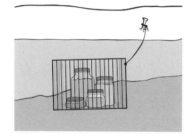

FIGURE 20: IMMERSION COOLING

COLD ROOM

A *cold room* is simply a room in your home that is kept as cold as possible. It should be on the shadiest side of the house, and it works best with some type of venting to the outside. Cold rooms can be as reliable as refrigerators for most of the year in cooler climates, and they are much more spacious.

A cold room functions similarly to a cold cellar, in that it uses passive convection. The warm air passes out the upper vents or holes and allows cool air to enter. These holes are opened in the evening when it becomes cool, and are closed in the morning. However, since a cold room is above ground, it cannot rely on the cool temperature of the earth. For this reason, your cold room can be made more effective by adding objects with a large amount of thermal mass, such as bricks, stone blocks, or large containers or barrels of water.

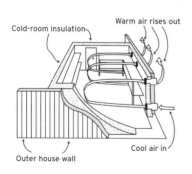

FIGURE 21: A SIMPLE COLD ROOM

VAPOR PANTRIES AND POT-IN-POT COOLERS

The following two techniques work by using the method of *evaporative cooling*. This is essentially the same process in which our bodies release sweat to cool us down.

You can build a simple *vapor pantry* by using a container, preferably one that is waterproof, such as a small cupboard, or a barrel with an access door cut in one side. Place a tray of water on top of the container. Place the center of a large damp towel, or the attached edges of several smaller towels, in the tray, using a weight to hold that part of the towel beneath the waterline. Let the rest of the towels hang over the sides of the container. The water in the tray will be wicked into the towels, keeping them damp. As the water evaporates, it will cool the cabinet and the contents stored inside.

Water container

The *pot-in-pot cooler* was recently adapted and popularized by Mohammed Bah Abba, an innovative Nigerian professor who has been lauded for his contribution to the preservation of perishable food in countries with arid climates. The technique is very simple. Place one earthenware pot inside a larger earthenware pot. Fill the space between them with wet sand and make sure the sand stays continuously moist, thereby keeping the outer pot damp. Place items to be kept cool in the inner pot, and cover the top of the pots with a wet cloth. The water contained in the sand between the pots is wicked toward and evaporates from the outer surface of the larger pot, which moves heat out of the cooler. The outside pot must be unglazed so that water can evaporate through it more easily, but the inside pot can be glazed.

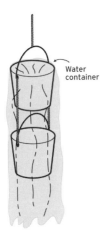

Water container

FIGURE 22b:
TWO-BUCKET EVAPORATION COOLER

Both techniques work best in relatively dry and well-ventilated—preferably windy—areas. You can try placing these cooling devices outside in the shade, so that they are exposed to more wind. Alternatively, you can put a device that works by evaporation in the wall of your house, so that you can access the food from inside and protect it from scavengers, but let the wind outside help with the cooling.

You can also use a system with two buckets—one full of water, and the other full of food. This can be hung from a shady tree, with the water bucket on top. A cloth is draped over both buckets, with part of it immersed in the water. This method works much the same way as the cabinet-style evaporation cooler.

SALVAGED AND MODIFIED REFRIGERATORS

It is possible to modify some refrigeration equipment so that it is powered directly by a motive force other than electricity. I have seen a chest freezer that functions quite well with the compressor energized by a water wheel, using no electricity. However, this wouldn't be appropriate for most people, so I won't go into more detail here.

Another type of refrigerator that would be appropriate for salvaging is the ammonia-using type used in recreational vehicles (RVs). This type has no moving parts and runs on heat from burning propane gas. It works by alternating between a heating phase, in which a mixture of ammonia and water is heated to boil out the ammonia, and a cooling phase in which ammonia and water recombine, a reaction that takes heat from the surrounding atmosphere. It could be modified to run off a fire created by wood, biodigested methane, or any other source of sufficient heat. A refrigerator working on this principle could even be solar-powered. For more information on ammonia-type refrigerators used in RVs, see http://www.nh3tech.org/absorption.html, or a manual on refrigeration.

Cooling References
- *The Encyclopedia of Country Living,* by Carla Emery (8th Edition, Sasquatch Books, 1994)
- *Fieldbook for Canadian Scouting,* Boy Scouts of Canada, 1986

PART 5

Heat for Cooking

CHAPTER 17

SOME BASICS ABOUT HEAT AND COOKING

THERE ARE A FEW BASIC concepts involved in cooking and in designing cookers that will cook as rapidly, efficiently, and conveniently as possible. As with cooling systems, there are three essential concepts that relate to cooking: heat gain, heat loss, and heat storage.

Heat gain is the heat that enters a cooker from solar energy, either by direct sunlight, or through the solar energy released by burning wood and other potential fuels. Heat loss is heat that escapes by heat movement. (This process is described in detail in chapter 12.)

When cooking with wood fires, remember that smoke is uncombusted fuel. A very efficient fire is almost smokeless, which means that fuel and trees are being conserved and that air pollution is minimized. To make a fire efficient, strive to keep its temperature as high as possible, above 1100° F (600° C). This means regulating and warming the supply of air, if possible. It may also mean insulating the combustion chamber, and using low-mass materials for building the stove so that the heat is contained and concentrated. Low-mass materials may include a steel combustion chamber rather than a brick one (see the section on the rocket stove, page 61, for more specific information).

In general, you can save a lot of cooking fuel (and cooking time) by cutting food into small pieces, grinding up grains, presoaking dried beans overnight, and using minimal water. Food cooks more quickly when steamed, rather than boiled, because water absorbs much of the heat. Always use a lid when cooking to contain the heat inside the pot.

A HAYBOX IS AN INSULATED container that can yield significant fuel savings—up to 70 percent. Simply bring food to a boil, place the hot cooking pot inside a haybox, and cover the box. The haybox will contain the heat in the food so that it will continue cooking without using extra fuel. A haybox works by maximizing heat storage and minimizing heat loss. This device is ideal for foods with a high water content like soups, stews, rice, boiled eggs, and such. Foods that lose a lot of steam on a stove can be cooked with less water using a haybox.

When using a haybox for recipes with beans or legumes, like chili, you should precook the beans and legumes to make them safe to eat by boiling them on your stove or fire for ten to fifteen minutes. Then add the other ingredients before placing the pot into your haybox.

Hayboxes can also be used to raise bread or to incubate yogurt or tempeh, a fermented soybean product. Place a container of hot water in the haybox along with the dough, yogurt, or soybeans to maintain a warm temperature.

You can make a haybox from all sorts of local materials, such as a basket filled with dried grass and covered with a bag or pillowcase of dried grass on top. You can also use a cooler as part of a haybox, but you will probably want to add more insulation. You can open the haybox to check on cooking progress, but you will lose a tiny amount of heat each time you do this. If you forget to take your food out of the haybox, or if you overestimate the time, the food may be cooked more than you intended, but it will not burn.

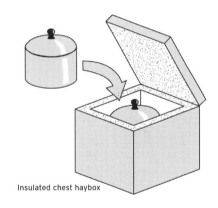

Insulated chest haybox

FIGURE 23: HAYBOXES

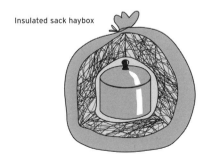

Insulated sack haybox

CHART 3: HAYBOX COOKING TIMES

FOOD	BOIL TIME	HAYBOX TIME
Rice	5 minutes	1–1.5 hours
Potatoes	5 minutes	1–2 hours
Soup and Stock	10 minutes	2–3 hours
Green Lentils	10 minutes	3–4 hours
Pintos	10 minutes	3 hours
Split Peas	10 minutes	2 hours
Quinoa	5 minutes	1.5 hours
Millet	5 minutes	1 hour
Winter Squash	5 minutes	1–2 hours
Steamed Bread	30 minutes	3 hours
Polenta	1 minute	1 hour
Chicken	6 minutes	2–3 hours
Beef	13 minutes	3–4 hours

Haybox References

- *Aprovecho's Guide to Hayboxes and Fireless Cooking*, by Peter Scott, et al. Aprovecho Research Center (www.aprovecho.net)
- *Fireless Cooking,* by Heidi Kirschner (Madrona Publishers, 1981)

BY USING FUEL-EFFICIENT WOODSTOVES, we can save fuel, trees, and time spent gathering wood, as well as reduce air pollution. Stove efficiency is based on two main factors. First, an efficient stove converts as much of the energy in the wood as possible into heat. Second, an efficient stove transfers as much of the heat as possible into the food being cooked. If we say that a given stove is 10 percent efficient, that means 10 percent of the energy in the burning wood goes into the food.

Not all woodstoves are very efficient. Some lose enormous amounts of heat by heating up large metal bodies, which then lose more heat to the ground and air around them. If you want to boil a 4-pound (2 kg) pot of beans, there is no need to heat up 600 pounds of steel as well.

We will look at open fires, which can be between 8 percent and 18 percent efficient, or better, depending on the skill of the fire builder, the type of fire, and the wind conditions. We will also look at the rocket stove, which can be more than 24 percent efficient, and the Dona Justa stove, which can be more than 40 percent efficient. Please exercise caution when building fires or stoves.

OPEN FIRES

To build a fire, start with very fine, dry pieces of flammable materials called tinder. This could include moss, shredded paper, birch or cedar bark, or wood shavings. This material is the easiest to light. On top of that, loosely stack somewhat larger materials, known as kindling, such as pencil-diameter sticks and twigs, or rolled-up newspaper. On top of that, place large pieces of wood— the fuel. To aid in starting a fire, you may want to make some tinder that is attached to a larger fuel source. To create a "fuzz stick," take a knife to a stick as if you were making wood shavings, but leave the shavings attached at one end. In very wet weather, you can split open a log that is dry inside, and make "fuzz" from the interior.

There are two easy ways to stack materials for a fire: log cabin–style or tipi-style. A log cabin pile has the tinder at the bottom inside, and the kindling stacked crisscrossed. In a tipi-style fire, the sticks are leaned into each other, or some are positioned with their ends stuck into the ground for stability. One advantage of the tipi-style fire is that the sticks will fall into the fire as it burns.

FIGURE 24a: LOG CABIN-STYLE FIRE STARTER

FIGURE 24b: TIPI-STYLE FIRE STARTER

FIGURE 24c: THREE-STONE FIRE

For both types, you need to leave spaces for airflow. Fire making is a skill that takes practice, and you'll improve over time.

If you have long logs for fuel, don't waste time and energy sawing or chopping them. Just put three large stones around a fire to reflect and retain heat, and then insert the ends of the logs in between the stones. As the logs burn, push them in further and further, until they are completely burned.

Cooking on an Open Fire

There are numerous ways to cook on an open fire. You can place a grill on top of the fire and cook meat or vegetables. You can place pots or pans on a grill. You can also hang pots from a "crane" or "spit." Just drive two forked sticks into the ground, and place another stick between them. It's also possible to build up a coal bed, rake coals out of the fire, and then cook meat or vegetables directly on the coals.

In highly improvised circumstances, you can make a hole in the ground and line it with some type of waterproof membrane. Place water and food to cook within the hole. Heat clean rocks in an open fire and then drop them into the water or stew so that it boils. You can also wrap food, such as potatoes, in aluminum foil, and place it near the fire or in the coals. You can even bury aluminum-wrapped food in the coals of a fire and cook it overnight. If you don't have foil, you can remove the tops from two aluminum cans, place the food inside one can, and then jam the other over it as a cover.

Another improvised way of cooking is to make a fire in a pit and burn it down to a coal bed. You may want to place rocks inside as well. Cover the coals with a thick layer of nonpoisonous leaves. Then put on a layer of the food you want to cook, then another layer of leaves, and then soil or sand as a cover. The heat and steam will be trapped inside, cooking your food.

One final note of caution: Never use rocks from a riverbed (or other wet area) to place in or near your fire. There may be water trapped inside the rocks, which could reach a boiling temperature and cause the rocks to explode.

Hearth Variations

The efficiency of an open fire drops significantly when it is windy. There are several ways to deal with that situation. You can lay two logs parallel to each other along opposite sides of the fire, or make a U-shaped hearth with rocks. Wind blowing into the hearth will feed the fire with air. You can also dig a shallow trench a few feet long, about a foot deep, and wide enough for your pots to straddle the opening. A similar style of hearth can be made by stacking bricks or similar materials into that same trough shape.

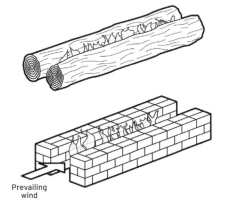

Prevailing wind

FIGURE 25: HEARTH EXAMPLES

A fire technique that is bit more elaborate, and probably the best style for high winds, is to make a fire hole. Dig a U-shaped hole, and start a fire in one end. You can feed fuel through the other side of the hole. Place your pot, elevated on sticks to allow airflow, over the side with the fire.

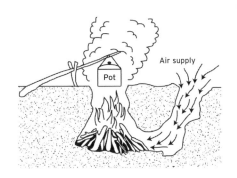

Air supply

Pot

FIGURE 26: FIRE HOLE

IMPROVISED WOODSTOVES

There are many designs for improvised stoves. Some are better than others. For example, you can make a very simple stove with a metal paint can. Remove the lid, and punch several large holes in the body of the can at the bottom of one side and the top of the other. Start the fire inside the can. Turn the side with the holes on the bottom into the wind and place your pot on top.

Among the more efficient improvised stove designs are two developed by the Aprovecho Research Center, in Cottage Grove, Oregon.

Rocket Stove

Designed by Dr. Larry Winiarski, this excellent stove incorporates several design principles:

- The Insulation around the fire keeps the fire burning hot (above 1100° F or 600° C), which is highly efficient.

- Insulation around the chimney increases the draft, which provides a constant supply of air.

- Low-mass materials are burned, so that the heat produced is absorbed by the food being cooked instead of by the stove.

- Wood burns at the tip, and is shoved into the fire, controlling the burn rate and reducing smoke.

- The air-fuel mixture is controlled, since too much air will cool the fire.

- A skirt around the pot maximizes heat contact and transfer into the food.

- Cooking occurs directly on top of the chimney and results in efficient heat transfer. This is possible because the stove burns at high temperatures and is nearly smokeless.

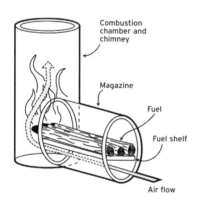

FIGURE 27a: ROCKET STOVE ELBOW

The rocket stove is a versatile design that can be improvised with various materials. The heart of the stove is an elbow-shaped, insulated combustion chamber. Fuel, in the form of sticks or narrow pieces of wood (or even tightly rolled-up paper, if that's all you have), is fed into the fire on a shelf in the lower arm of the elbow. Air enters into the fire underneath this shelf. Because the combustion chamber is insulated, the fire can get very hot and burn very efficiently.

To build a rocket stove, you will need a housing container, such as a coffee can. For the housing container, you may want to choose a size which is large enough to support the pot to be used, but the design is adaptable and can vary in size. Make a hole in the larger can in which to insert the elbow chamber. For the stove elbow (a vertical combustion chamber and chimney connected to a horizontal magazine-style feed for fuel), you can use stovepipe, scrap metal, or a pair of cans put one into the other. (An improvised can chamber will last for about three months. Plastering the inside with castable firebrick will improve the lifespan. A taller chimney will be more smokeless. However, a shorter chimney will let the flame touch the bottom of the pot, and transfer heat more efficiently to the food.)

Place the elbow joint inside the housing container. You may need to place a brick or other material underneath to help maintain the placement. Then fill the space between the elbow and the housing with fireproof insulation. This insulation could include dry wood ash, vermiculite, perlite, pumice rock, dead coral, or air-trapping layers of aluminum foil.

You will need to make a shelf for the fuel wood to place within the elbow joint. You can pound a can flat, and cut it to fit. A small, adjustable control door on the end of the elbow will allow you to adjust airflow to the fire and change how fast the fuel burns. You may want to

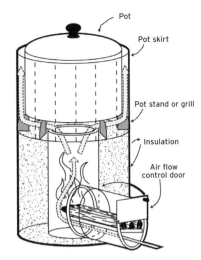

FIGURE 27b: FULL ASSEMBLY OF ROCKET STOVE

make a wire grill to place on top of the housing as a support for a pot.

Adding a metal skirt around the pot, made from sheet metal, aluminum foil, or other fireproof and malleable material, will also aid the heat transfer tremendously, because it will force the hot gases to rub against more of the pot, as shown. The skirt should be about a half-inch (1 cm) from the pot.

Starting a rocket stove is slightly different than starting an open fire. First put your tinder on the shelf, ignite it, and then push the fuel inside.

Dona Justa Stove

Another Aprovecho stove design, the Dona Justa stove, is an extension of the rocket stove concept. Designed for indoor use, it includes a long chimney that

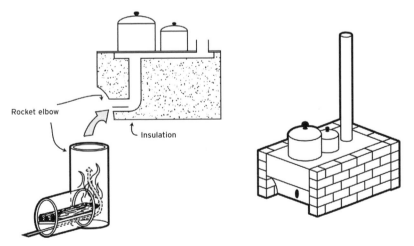

FIGURE 28a: SIMPLE FLAT-TOP DONA JUSTA STOVE   **FIGURE 28b:** ASSEMBLED

vents the minimal amount of smoke produced to the outside. The chimney should be made from stovepipe, if available, although other metal tubes can be used. Hot gases from the combustion chamber move up and across the bottom of a metal cooking surface. The underside of this passage is insulated to retain heat. The smoke then goes up the chimney and outside.

The simplest form of this stove is the one shown in Figure 28a. The stove is essentially a box (made out of brick, compressed clay, or other similar non-flammable material) filled with insulation of the same type used in the rocket stove discussed previously (dry wood ash, vermiculite, etc.). The rocket stove combustion chamber is placed in the front of this box and gases flow through a shallow metal channel which is laid on the top of the insulation. A front plate made from metal helps to keep the combustion chamber and insulation in place. A sheet-metal cooking surface is placed on top of the channel and the walls of the box and fits tightly to retain hot gases. Cooking pots are placed on top of this metal sheet.

The downside of this stove, in terms of efficiency, is that the metal cooking surface will release heat into the air wherever it is not touching a pot. You can improve the efficiency of this stove by making holes in the surface so that the pots can be put into the channel where the hot gases travel (see a cross section of this in Figure 28c). This contact improves heat transfer. You can build a form-fitting channel, as shown, so that the gases are forced to go as tightly as possible against the pots. Figure 28d provides a three-dimensional perspective, and Figure 28e may give you a better idea of the various parts of the Dona Justa stove and how they fit together. Although the insulation is shown in the shape it becomes in the assembled stove, it is loose and should be put into the stove after the walls have already been erected.

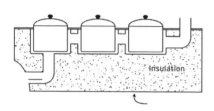

FIGURE 28c: POT-INSET, CROSS SECTION

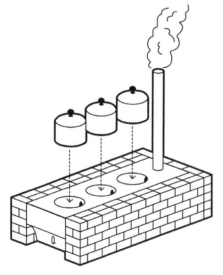

FIGURE 28d: POT-INSET, VARIATION
ASSEMBLED

This stove is more sophisticated than the rocket stove, and it helps if you have someone who has built the stove before to assist you in its construction. However, a person or group with good general building skills can make a well-constructed stove.

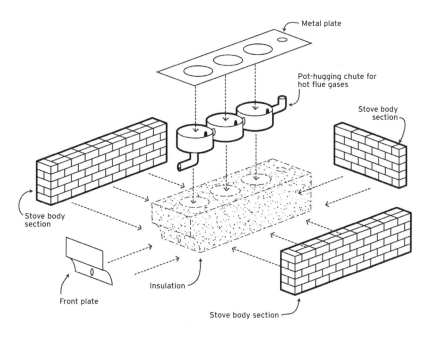

Metal plate

Pot-hugging chute for
hot flue gases

Stove body
section

Stove body
section

Insulation

Front plate

Stove body section

FIGURE 28e: DONA JUSTA STOVE VARIATION ELEMENTS

| SOLAR COOKING

HEAT GAIN IN SOLAR COOKING comes from a few main sources:

- *The greenhouse effect,* by which light travels though glass or transparent plastic and hits objects inside, but the heat is unable to get back out through the glass.

- *Glass orientation* (glazing) allows more light to travel though the glass if it is at a right angle to the incoming light. Otherwise, part of the light will reflect away from the solar collector.

- *Reflectors* direct more light toward the pot or oven.

There are many types of creative solar collectors for use in cooking, and I encourage you to check out various types to see what might work best for you.

TIPS FOR SOLAR COOKING

Here are some suggestions for using the sun's energy in cooking.

- Use dark pots with lids.

- Don't open the pot while cooking. The temperature is lower than in other types of cooking, so you generally don't need to stir because sticking and burning is rare.

- Get an early start, because solar cooking takes longer than other sorts of cooking.

- Adjust the solar cooker regularly to follow the sun.

- If you double the scale of a solar cooker design, you increase the amount of light captured by a factor of four.

To make solar reflectors, use whatever materials you have available. For example, you can paste aluminum foil onto corrugated cardboard. Contact cement works well as an adhesive. When using aluminum foil, make sure to use the shiny side and not the matte (dull) side. Also, make sure that the foil is placed on smoothly; wrinkles will impair the focus so that less of the reflected light reaches the target. You can also use polished sheet aluminum, other polished sheet metals, or aluminized Mylar.

SIMPLE FOLDING SOLAR COOKER

This is the simplest, most portable, and lowest-temperature solar cooker of the designs described in this book. It can be built quickly and easily using basic materials, such as aluminum foil smoothly pasted onto corrugated cardboard. It will work well on brighter days or in sunnier latitudes, but the lack of insulation and small size of the reflectors means that it will not be as effective as some of the following designs are in less-favorable conditions. This and other solar cooker designs can be used for cooking as well as to boil or disinfect water for safety, a process described in chapter 7.

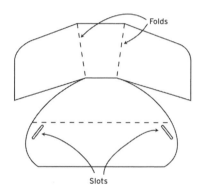

FIGURE 29a: PATTERN FOR FOLDING SOLAR COOKER

This design is fairly forgiving and does not have to be constructed exactly as shown. Use the basic pattern shown to make a cardboard sheet in the appropriate shape and then adhere aluminum foil smoothly onto the surface. Make the three folds shown, and cut the two slots into the lower portion of the pattern. Fold the two upper "wings" so that their ends fit into the slots and the bottommost portion of the pattern folds up off of the ground.

If you place a black pot in a clear plastic bag, as shown, you will have better heat retention. A simple wire frame (made from coat-hanger wire or other available stiff wire) can prevent the bag from touching the pot and melting on it. It will also keep the pot off of the ground, reducing heat loss from conduction of heat into the earth.

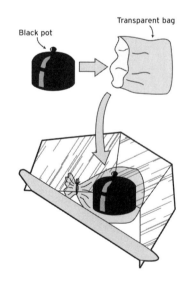

FIGURE 29b: INCREASING HEAT RETENTION IN FOLDING SOLAR COOKER

SOLAR OVEN

The next simplest solar design is derived from the work of Dr. Maria Telkes, a chemist and pioneering inventor of solar-energy technologies (including the first residential solar heating system, which she designed in 1948). To design this oven, you will need a protractor or an improvised means of determining angles (see Appendix B: Useful Tools and Materials).

This solar oven requires a small piece of glass, which can be salvaged from any number of sources. Choose the size of the glass pane to suit the size of your oven, but about 24 by 18 inches (60 by 45 cm) is a good approximate size for a larger oven. Then you'll need to make an insulated box to house the glass. The top of the box is an angled window, and the back has a door to access the food.

You can use plywood for the main structure of the box, or any other improvised material that you can work with, including plank wood or metal. You can even use corrugated cardboard if you don't mind keeping the oven out of the rain. Line the inside of the box with a sheet of metal.

Between the housing and the metal, place approximately 1 inch (3 cm) of insulation. For improvised insulation in this solar oven, you can use alternating layers of aluminum foil and corrugated cardboard. You can also use wood ash, charcoal, and such.

To decide the ideal angle of the glass for this cooker (as well as in the solar still described on page 23) take your latitude and subtract it from the number 90. This is the noontime average annual angle of the sun in the sky. Add 23.5 to get the sun's noontime angle on the summer solstice, and subtract 23.5 to get the sun's noontime angle at winter solstice. Pick the best angle, considering that the glass would ideally be positioned at an angle of 90 degrees to the sun. If you mostly cook in the summer, then you will want to use an angle between your average and summer solstice noontime angles.

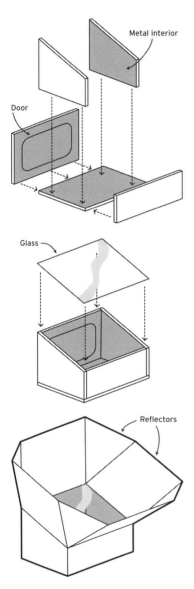

FIGURE 30a: SOLAR OVEN

Ideally, the interior of a solar oven is lined with black-painted metal so that it absorbs as much light as possible and then turns it into heat. Use water-based paint. (Before using your oven, let it bake empty in the sun for two days to get rid of harmful gases from the paint.) If you don't have black paint, you can improvise by suspending the metal panels over smoke from a fire or lamp so that one side of the metal becomes blackened. Historically soot from lamps and candles, known as *lampblack*, was collected and mixed with linseed oil, turpentine, and varnish to make black paint.

Then, mount reflective panels as shown to reflect the sunlight into the oven. An angle of about 30 degrees from the sun (or 120 degrees from the glass), as shown, works best. To make reflectors with those angles, construct two simple rectangular reflectors and two rectangular reflectors with triangular "wings." The triangles should be the shape depicted, with the outer two angles at 66 degrees and the inner angle at 48 degrees. This layout will provide optimal capture of sunlight. You can use corrugated cardboard with aluminum foil, as discussed previously, but you may want to use several layers of cardboard, with the corrugations running perpendicular, to make the reflectors as strong as possible. The best reflectivity and greatest strength would be obtained from using sections of mirror mounted on plywood.

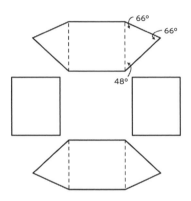

FIGURE 30b: SOLAR OVEN, REFLECTORS LAID OUT FLAT

The exact dimensions of the rectangular portions will depend on the size of your box. The larger the reflectors are (that is, the farther they extend out from where they meet the box), the more effective your oven will be. However, large reflectors may also make the oven harder to move or more likely to catch the wind and become damaged. The optimal size depends on your location, but at least 2 to 3 feet (60 to 100 cm) in length is a good range to start with.

It's best to have a relatively easy way to adjust the position of the collector to follow the sun. The oven illustrated is simply mounted on skids, which sit on the ground so that the oven can be slid or rotated easily by one person. You'll probably want to adjust it about every fifteen minutes or so. Experiment to see what works best for you.

PARABOLIC COOKER

The parabolic cooker is a bit more complicated, but it works well if you can manage it. You can even fry on a parabolic cooker. Here we will look at the basic concept, as well as a few variations.

FIGURE 31a: PARABOLIC HOT
WATER HEATER

The basis of the parabolic cooker is the parabola, a curve that reflects incoming parallel rays (such as from the sun) onto a small point. This permits very high temperatures to be created. For this reason, there is an important warning: do not look directly into the reflected sunlight inside the reflector. This could cause severe eye damage. For safety, make sure to put the focal point inside the cup of the reflector.

You can draw a *parabola* using a right-angled ruler or framing square without any knowledge of mathematics. (Geometrically, a parabola is defined as a curve on which any point is the same distance from the focal point as it is from a baseline, known as the *directrix*.) You will also need a nail and a rectangular piece of cardboard (or similar material) with the bottom cut along a straight line.

Place the nail where you would like the focal point to be. This will be somewhere in the bottom half of the cardboard and centered between right and left. Always keep one arm of the framing square against the nail and the outside corner along the baseline. Start with the corner directly below the nail. Move the corner a little bit away from the center each time and draw a line from the baseline out toward the edge of the cardboard. Eventually you will have many lines that intersect along a curve. This thick composite curve is your parabola.

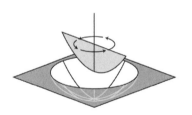

FIGURE 31b: TURNING A
PARABOLA IN CLAY
TO MAKE A MOLD
FOR REFLECTORS

If you want, you can use the concave (or cave-shaped) section of the parabola as a frame template for a solar collector, as pictured in Figure 31b. This is appropriate for heating water, or for cooking hot dogs or shish kabobs. However, you may lose a lot of heat as the food is cooked, since it is exposed and has a large surface area. Sheltering the collector from the wind and insulating the side of the food facing away from the collector can reduce this loss.

If you use the convex section of the parabola (the part with the curve extending outward), you can simply rotate it in clay to produce a mold. To do this you will need to make your parabola stronger than with just cardboard, such as by tracing and cutting it from plywood. The clay will allow you to make a very good parabolic surface to place aluminum foil on, but using a solid block of clay would be quite heavy. A more convenient option is to place a layer of clay onto a dish-shaped or roughly parabolic framework of woven or lashed-together sticks.

You will also need to build a base on which to mount the reflector to rotate it to follow the sun, and a pot holder, such as a grill attached to a rod or

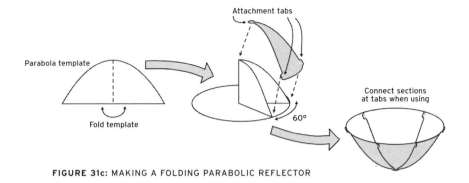

Attachment tabs

Parabola template

Connect sections
at tabs when using

Fold template

60°

FIGURE 31c: MAKING A FOLDING PARABOLIC REFLECTOR

spit. Also, an alignment indicator will help you to line up your parabolic cooker with the sun. To make an alignment indicator, place a nail or post vertically on a small flat surface, such as a plywood disk. Mount the indicator on the side of the cooker that directly faces the sun. When the nail or post casts no shadow, the collector is properly aligned.

You can also make a folding reflector. It will not be a true parabola in all three dimensions, but will be close enough for cooking and is much more portable. This reflector is best suited for thin, polished sheet metal or foil on a non-corrugated cardboard backing, since the reflectors must be curved.

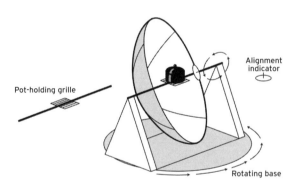

Alignment
indicator

Pot-holding grille

Rotating base

FIGURE 31d: PARABOLIC SOLAR
REFLECTOR

First, make a cardboard parabola. Fold the parabola in half, symmetrically, along the midline. This will act as your template for several identical wedge-shaped sections that will make up your parabola.

Before making these wedges you will need to decide how many sections you want to include. The more sections you have, the more accurate the focus of the reflector will be—but it will also be more difficult to make and have more potential places to fall apart.

When you fold the template, make the angle of your fold appropriate to the size of material you have available, but make sure that it will divide evenly into a circle. For instance, if you want to make a folding collector with six segments, divide 360° by six (to get 60°) and angle the two halves of the template 60° apart. For eight segments, use 45°, and so on. Curve a piece of flexible cardboard (or your reflective material) over the curve of your folded template and cut it to fit (but leave extra material for tabs at the corners and sides). This new

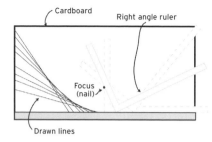

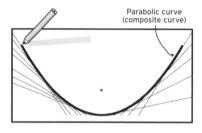

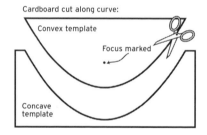

FIGURE 32: DRAWING A PARABOLA

pattern will be a new template for your wedge-shaped reflective sections.

Use this new pattern to trace and cut your reflective sections. When you have them all cut, stack them on top of each other and attach them together at the central tab. You can do this by driving a thumbtack or small screw or roofing nail through the center and into a piece of wood, rubber, or cork on the other side. Poke holes through all of the tabs at the outer edge. Then "fan out" the various sections to form a concave shape, as shown, so that the tabs overlap each other, and use string or wire (such as from paper clips) strung through the holes in the tabs to hold the reflector's shape.

It's worth noting that satellite dishes are also parabolic reflectors used to capture radio waves. If you can find one of an appropriate size (and especially one that can be adjusted for tracking), you may be able to cover it with reflective material and use the existing structure.

You can make a parabolic reflector from numerous materials. Aluminum foil or polished metal will do, and mirror pieces are even better in terms of reflectivity (although cutting and attaching them is more difficult).

In general, collectors larger than 6.5 feet (2 meters) across are considered unwieldy, but you can manage it if you have a sturdy mounting and high winds are not likely to be a problem.

If a parabola is too difficult to construct, you can also make a simple conical cooker for boiling water. Cut a circle out of sheet metal or cardboard. To make a circle, first place a nail in the center of your sheet with a string the length of the desired radius of your circle. Then tie a pencil or sharp nail at the loose end of the string, and move it around the reach of the string to draw the circle. Using a protractor, measure a segment of the circle that is 105.5° and cut away that segment, after drawing in two tables along one side of the section to be removed. If you use cardboard, then glue aluminum foil onto the remaining section of the circle. Bring the edges together to form a cone.

The focus of the conical collector is a line along the center of the cone. You can use a black pipe filled with water as the container, or make a long black metal sleeve and put the kettle into the top. You can make the reflector as large as you desire, practically speaking. The black pipe or sleeve should be long enough to reach the top of the reflector when viewed from the side (see Figure 33b), but the diameter is not crucial. Just remember that larger volumes of water will, of course, take more time to heat up.

To make a black metal sleeve, paint one side of a piece of sheet metal black and then bend that metal into a cylinder. To retain that shape, you may want to overlap the edges slightly and crimp them together firmly with pliers, and reinforce it by tying wire around the sleeve. Welding or soldering the joints would help to create a sturdier cylinder, if you have access to tools for those techniques.

Mount the sleeve or pipe onto a circular board, as shown (onto which you will also attach your conical reflector). L-brackets and screws or tight wire can help you to attach the mounting board to the sleeve. The mounting board should have a pipe or rod firmly fixed to its back surface. This will allow you to move the reflector to track the sun more easily. This rod can be put through holes in a supporting frame and clamped into place when the reflector is pointed in the correct direction.

This design can be scaled up or down in size to suit your needs.

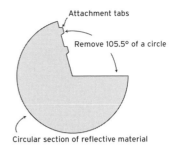

FIGURE 33a: CONICAL SOLAR COOKER

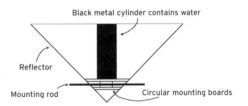

FIGURE 33b: CROSS SECTION OF ASSEMBLY
OF CONICAL COLLECTOR

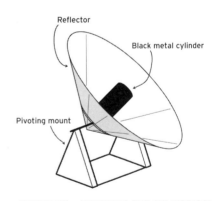

FIGURE 33c: MOUNTING THE CYLINDRICAL
CENTER

Solar Cooking References
- www.solarcooking.org
- "Capturing Heat" (Booklets One and Two), by Dean Still et al., Aprovecho Research Center (www.aprovecho.net)

BIODIGESTED METHANE

Methane produced by decomposition in a chamber may be a suitable source of cooking fuel in some situations. Essentially, cow manure, straw, and other organic materials with high *embodied-energy content* (substances that have a lot of potential energy stored within that could be released, for instance, by burning) are allowed to decompose under controlled circumstances. It's like composting, but without air. This may be a good option for people with limited access to firewood, but plenty of organic biomass materials available.

The subject is too extensive to cover thoroughly in this book, but you can find more information online, at sites such as http://www.builditsolar.com/Projects/BioFuel/biofuels.htm#Methane.

You can also refer to books like *Methane Digesters for Fuel Gas and Fertilizer, with Complete Instructions for Two Working Models,* by L. John Fry (The New Alchemy Institute, 1973), also available online at http://journeytoforever.org/biofuel_library/MethaneDigesters/MDToC.html.

| # OTHER COOKING OPTIONS

THERE ARE OTHER IMPROVISED COOKING measures that I have not covered here, largely because of their dependence on petroleum-derived fuels. However, some of those options can be excellent for temporary or emergency situations.

Semisolid fuels like paraffin, gelled alcohol, and Sterno cans are safe and easy to use, although they don't generally burn as hot as other sources. You can find gelled, spill-proof fuels in camping or hardware stores, sometimes sold as Canned Heat, or Warming Gel. Some environmentally friendly products are made from sugar cane byproducts. Liquid fuels like denatured alcohols or methyl hydrate can be used relatively safely in very simple improvised stoves.

For a quick improvised stove, you can use a simple shallow metal cup with a small amount of fuel alcohol, or a "plumber's stove"—a can filled with cotton balls and alcohol. For more information on alcohol-burning improvised stoves, see http://home.comcast.net/~agmann/stove/Stoves.htm.

Liquid fuels, such as kerosene and gasoline, can also be used for fuel. However, they are volatile and difficult to use safely since they can explode and produce dangerous gases in an enclosed area.

Also keep in mind that most grains and seeds can be prepared without cooking. Simply soak and sprout them. These sprouts can then be eaten raw. All you need is dried seeds or grains, clean water, and a place to sprout the seeds.

Place the seeds in a screen bag, a jar with a cloth over the mouth, or even a simple tray. Rinse the seeds in fresh water several times a day to keep them wet, and let the excess water drain off. In a few days the seeds will grow into sprouts.

Keep in mind that many beans, such as red kidney beans and soybeans, cannot be eaten safely without cooking, and that sprouting is only safe if clean drinking water is used. You can find more information about raw foods at websites such as www.living-foods.com.

References on Other Cooking Options:
- "Capturing Heat" (Booklets One and Two), by Dean Still et al., Aprovecho Research Center
- *The Aprovecho "Fish Camp" Stove Book,* by Dean Still.
  The Aprovecho Research Center website is www.aprovecho.net.
  Check out their stove page at http://aprovecho.net/at/atindex.htm.

- *Fieldbook for Canadian Scouting* (Boy Scouts of Canada, 1986)
- The Journey to Forever Woodstove page, http://journeytoforever.org/at_woodfire.html
- The Home-Made Stove Archives, at http://wings.interfree.it/html/main.html
- The extensive Renewable Energy Policy Project's Biomass Cooking Stoves page, http://www.repp.org/discussiongroups/resources/stoves/

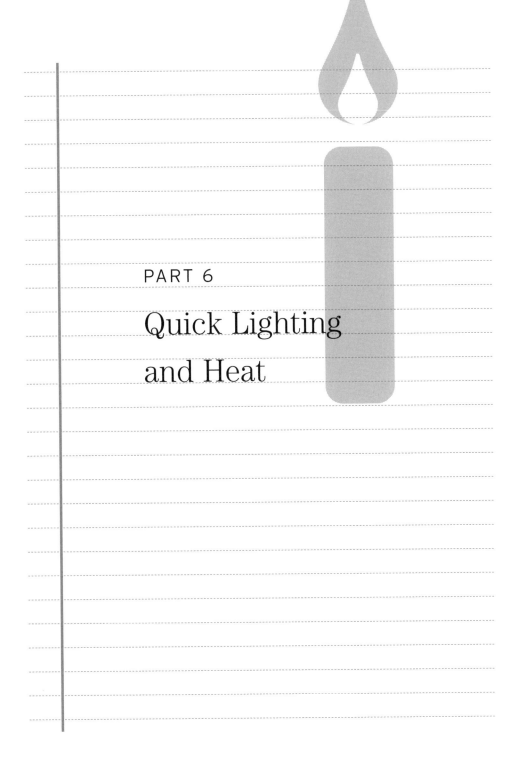

PART 6

Quick Lighting
and Heat

| # LIGHTING OPTIONS

IN THIS CHAPTER, WE'LL LOOK at lighting that does not rely on electricity. Some of these methods have been used for centuries; others are more contemporary innovations.

OIL LAMPS

The oil lamp is a very old form of lighting. The original oil lamps were often as simple as a cup or bowl partially filled with oil, with a wick that soaked up the oil and was lit. A wick can be as basic as a piece of twisted moss, cloth, or frayed rope. More or larger wicks result in more light.

You can use pottery to make oil lamps with more complex shapes. The general historical shape was much like a teakettle, with a cotton, hemp, or other fibrous wick coming out of the spout. The oil was poured in through the top. All sorts of oil and fat were used.

Some sources suggest that olive oil and sunflower oil are the best vegetable oils for lamps, and corn oil is the worst. Place a saucer beneath an oil lamp to catch drips. Although the part of the lamp in contact with the flame will be hot, the rest of the lamp will be cool enough to touch.

You can also make a relatively safe improvised oil lamp, derived from a design in Cresson Kearney's *Nuclear War Survival Skills* (available online at: http://www.oism.org/nwss/). Take a glass jar and wrap wire around the mouth to form a handle. If you make a loop of wire at the top, the lamp can also be hung. Then find or make a small wooden float with a hole drilled through the middle. Place the wick through the hole. First, pour in a layer of water; this will raise

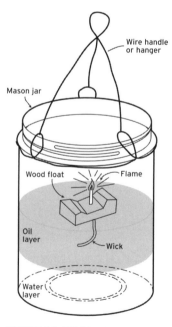

FIGURE 34: IMPROVISED OIL LAMP

the level of the oil to make it easier to light the wick without having to fill the entire jar with oil. Then pour in the layer of oil, place the float and wick, and light the lamp.

CANDLES

For a long time, Europeans made tallow candles for their lighting. Tallow is simply rendered animal fat, from which meat and other impurities have been removed by way of melting and straining. In the rendering process, fatty animal tissue is boiled and then cooled. The layer of fat that forms on the surface of the water is then scooped off and used for fuel.

To remove all impurities from tallow, you may need to boil the fat-water mixture, strain it, and then boil again repeatedly. After the mixture has been boiled, let it sit and cool. If you can get it cold enough, the fat will solidify and you can remove it in a block and pick off any remaining meat from the bottom. Keep in mind that overheated fat may catch fire. Watch the rendering fat at all times, do not overheat, and keep a tight-fitting lid nearby to contain and extinguish the fire in an emergency.

After the boiling-and-straining process, wicks are dipped in and out of a heated vat of tallow. Historically, this was smelly, unpleasant, and difficult. It could take fifty coats to make an ample candle. Using a mold makes the process easier, but it increases the initial expense (currently about US$10 per one-candle mold). Compared to modern paraffin (petroleum-derived) candles, tallow candles smell bad, sputter and drip, produce sooty smoke, don't burn for very long, and melt easily at a low temperature (around 80° F or 27° C).

European colonists in North America found that the berries of bayberry or wax myrtle plants could be boiled to obtain wax, which had a preferable smell and could be added to the tallow mix. Adding wild ginger and other spices also help to make the smell more pleasant. Beeswax candles are preferable in smell and longevity, but it is difficult to harvest large amounts of wax.

To produce a larger amount of light than what is emitted by a single candle, place numerous candles in soil in a ceramic flowerpot, with a reflector projecting out of the soil and above candle level on one side. A plastic flowerpot is lighter, but also more likely to melt or burn if the flame touches it, so nonflammable glass or ceramic containers are definitely preferred.

RUSH LIGHTS

Another lighting option is the rush light or rush candle. Rushes—thin, cylindrical plants that grow in marshy areas—are cut at the base of the plant. Then the husks are removed to leave the soft inner pith, which is dipped in melted fat and then lit. These improvised torches burn very quickly.

BUDDY BURNERS

The Buddy Burner is a simple improvised candle or stove, which can be used for lighting or for heat. The housing is a tuna can or similar shallow fireproof container, with a cardboard spiral inside. Melted paraffin, or other fat, is poured in to saturate the cardboard. Once it is burning, more fat or wax can be placed on top, which will then melt and burn as well. Place this burner on the ground or on a hot pad, since the container will get quite hot when the contents are mostly burned away. Placing a wick in the center may help it to get started. This is an excellent way to burn up the ends or drippings of other candles.

REFLECTORS

In all of these cases, reflectors can be used to direct more usable light onto the desired area. Reflectors don't necessarily have to be shiny or mirrored, only light-colored. Reflectors are also a good, simple way of getting more light indoors. At my home in the winter, sunlight reflects off of the white snow, and then up through the windows and off the white ceiling, and very deep into the house. During the day in winter, it is just as bright as it is in the summer, without any source of artificial light.

To test your ability to rely on other sources of light besides electricity, you may want to try some of the following exercises and experiments. Of course, whenever you use lighting that has a flame, make sure that you have firefighting materials on hand.

Assuming that you live in a house, do you need to use artificial lighting during the day? If you were making candles for all your lighting, you would probably want to save energy by only using them at night. In your home or workspace, can you position reflectors or paint surfaces white, so that you don't need to use artificial light indoors during the day?

Can you improvise an oil lamp or candle from materials that you can find in your home? What oils do you find work best? Would these oils be more valuable for food and cooking or for lighting? What materials work best for the wick? Is the smoke that is produced excessive or sooty? How can changing the wick or configuration improve those properties? What works well as a reflector? Experiment and have fun. Let us know what you find out. Contact us at editorial@inthewake.org.

As the culmination of these exercises, try taping all of the light switches in your house in the off position for a week. Use only reflected sunlight during the day, and only home-produced candles or oil lamps at night. How does this change your daily routine? Are there some tasks that you can only do during the day? Do you go to bed and get up earlier? Does it affect how you feel?

A word of caution: please be extremely careful when you use candles and oil lamps, and never leave them burning unattended. Always keep firefighting materials within easy reach.

OTHER SOURCES OF LIGHTING

Obviously, in most situations a flashlight would be safer and simpler, although not as long-lasting in some cases. You can buy flashlights that charge by solar power, cranking, or shaking, which are suitable for off-the-grid use. You can also make a fairly simple improvised electrical system from car parts and scavenged household electronics; however, this requires some understanding of the basic principles of electricity.

IN THIS CHAPTER, WE'LL FOCUS on a few simple strategies for staying warm. These can be used in emergency situations, and will provide ways to become less dependent on fossil fuel–based heating sources.

A Dona Justa stove or other efficient, improvised stove can be used to heat a house. Simply replace a window with a metal sheet, and run the stovepipe through it. However, if you burn anything larger than candles indoors, be sure to provide adequate ventilation. Try opening a window a crack on each side of a room, to avoid carbon monoxide poisoning. If you feel drowsy or have a headache, your body could be warning you of inadequate ventilation.

When burning a fire indoors, someone should always stay awake to make sure that it does not get out of hand, and to ensure that ventilation is adequate. Keep firefighting materials at hand, such as buckets of water or sand, baking soda, salt, a heavy blanket or tarp, or a chemical fire extinguisher.

To retain body heat, wear as much extra clothing as you can comfortably wear, and use extra blankets on your bed. Sleep close to other people and animals.

You can also make thermal curtains, which are essentially thick blankets, to hang over your windows (or you can hang layers of plastic over the windows to achieve the same effect). This will reduce heat loss, especially at night. Try to find drafts and block them, but do not make your house airtight. You need some air circulating from inside to outside to remove carbon dioxide and other gases that might build up and become toxic.

In an emergency, choose one room to concentrate the heat in, and close off the others. You can use partitions made out of blankets, drapes, cardboard, plywood, or several layers of plastic sheeting. Pick a room on the side of the house away from prevailing winds, and one that is well insulated and has few (or small) windows. An interior bathroom may work well, unless you are using a stove, in which case you need a window to vent. A basement may be a good choice, since the earth is somewhat warmer than the surface air in winter and has an insulating effect.

If you live in a cold climate and have to go without heat in your house, you will gradually get used to it. The colder temperatures will become more comfortable. (After spending six weeks in a tent on a mountainside late one winter, room temperature in a house felt uncomfortably hot to me.)

In cold weather, make sure to drink enough water. Cold air is relatively dry, and you may not be aware that you are becoming dehydrated. If you are slightly dehydrated, your metabolism slows significantly. You will probably need to eat more fat and calories as well, to ensure that your body has enough energy to keep itself warm.

Heating References
- "Staying Warm in an Unheated House: Coping With a Power Outage in Winter" (University of Wisconsin Extension, 1996)
- *The Encyclopedia of Country Living,* by Carla Emery (8th Edition, Sasquatch Books, 1994)

CONCLUSION

INDUSTRIAL COLLAPSE AND GRIDCRASH CAN be scary topics for most of us because we feel so ill prepared for them. People who have used earlier drafts of this book have told me that just reading it and having it at hand made them feel less anxious and more able to think seriously about these issues. I think this is especially important in the wake of events like Hurricane Katrina, and its impact on New Orleans, which showed us that serious gridcrash can happen to large numbers of people with minimal warning, and that governments aren't likely to respond effectively to that scale of disruption.

Learning these fundamental skills is a community activity, and I encourage you to practice them with others and discuss the related issues. I'm not as interested in "self-sufficiency" as I am in "community sufficiency." To be completely self-sufficient would be very difficult, time-consuming, improbable, and generally lonely. In contrast, if what I have to do is make sure that my community includes people with skills and experience, then my community sufficiency is relatively easy, time-saving, attainable, and much more fun and sociable.

It is sobering to realize that these skills will not be as helpful in a world that has been ecologically and socially obliterated by severe global warming and by resource wars. We cannot build healthy communities without a healthy land base.

Our challenges are large, but not insurmountable. If we work together to learn skills and help each other and our communities, we will not only survive: we could even thrive in the face of industrial collapse.

Appendix A and Appendix B

IF YOU LIVE IN A rural area, you may already take your own garbage and re-cyclables to a dump. But if you're an urban dweller, like most people in the industrialized world, your garbage is probably routinely collected by a waste management service.

There are many events that could disrupt that service. Industrial and economic collapse would obviously cause major disruptions, but strikes by service employees are also not uncommon. A long-term collapse in garbage collection would probably happen at the same time as a collapse in the consumption of disposable items, so this may not pose a significant problem for some people. However, skills for dealing with your own garbage or waste are still relevant today.

If you want to use resources wisely and efficiently, there are many ways to reuse materials that you would otherwise recycle industrially. I call these *remnant resources*—materials that an industrial society produces but that cannot be produced by ecological and egalitarian communities. These are re-sources that are available for now but will eventually run out because of use and degradation. In the meantime, here are some suggestions for how to han-dle various materials.

ORGANIC MATERIALS

Kitchen scraps and other organic materials can be composted to add to your garden, or simply returned to the earth. Compostable materials include paper products and other items made from natural materials, such as cotton and burlap.

PLASTICS

Plastic jars and bottles can, of course, be reused as containers. As described in chapter 6, PETE and HDPE containers are preferred for food and water storage.

Plastic soft-drink bottles, large ones in particular, can be used as irrigation systems for your garden. Tammy T., responding to my website, suggests poking about twenty small holes in a bottle and burying it so that only the mouth is visible. Plant them every few feet or so, depending on your soil and climate. Then you can fill them (with a funnel, if it helps) every few days; the water will gradually trickle directly to the roots of the plants.

Unfortunately, Tammy notes, plastic milk jugs are not well suited for this or other long-term storage uses. They tend to become cracked and brittle within about six months.

Plastic shopping bags are currently present in incredible numbers and if they are allowed to blow into the wild, they become a menace. However, they can be very useful for carrying things while they are intact. They can also be cut down the sides and included in shelter or clothing as improvised waterproofing or vapor barriers.

Melting shopping bags with a flame will yield an improvised hot glue or makeshift caulking. For instance, they can be used to seal the openings around pipes in the barrel of the slow sand filter described in chapter 8. They can also be made into cordage, such as ropes.

However, if there is any other option, Styrofoam and plastics should not be burned. In many cases, burning them releases a variety of toxic chemicals, including dioxin. So, while burning plastic rubbish is a way of getting rid of plastic where you are, it simply spreads the pollution into the air and water, where it cannot be contained. If certain plastics are no longer useful, put them in a dry, out-of-the-way place and store them indefinitely. One situation where it may be appropriate to incinerate plastics is in the disposal of contagious medical waste. However, never burn plastic inside a building or in a poorly ventilated area, since the gases produced are harmful.

METAL
You can reuse steel cans for many purposes, including using them as cooking stoves, pots, and storage containers. If you have no aluminum foil, remove the tops of two cans, place cut vegetables inside of them, jam them together, and cook the container in the fire. Non-enameled types may rust over time, depending on storage conditions. However, aluminum cans, including most beer cans, will not rust. Thus, they are good for storing water. To make waterproof and long-lasting improvised shingles, slit aluminum cans down the side and flatten them out.

GLASS
Glass jars and bottles can be used as containers and will last a long time. Thick glass can be used for knapping, the process of chipping to create arrowheads or other tools.

PAPER AND CARDBOARD
Paper and cardboard can be used for stove fuel. They can also be used for mulching and composting, but use only papers printed with black-and-white,

soy-based inks. Color inks and other types of ink include toxins that you don't want to introduce to the soil. Layers of corrugated cardboard make an effective insulation, as do layers of newspaper stuffed into clothing, although both are flammable.

POLYCOAT

Tetrapaks and other modern packaging often consist of multiple layers of plastic, foil, and paper, called polycoat. Disposing of polycoat can pose a challenge. Your best option is to try to reuse the containers. However, many people I know simply burn off the plastic and paper, and fish the foil out of the ashes.

For more general information on this topic, see my DIY Recycling page at http://inthewake.org/howtos/diy-recycling.html.

TOOLS AND MATERIALS:

A number of the devices in this book require—or can be constructed much more easily with—very basic skills in carpentry, plumbing, and metal shaping (for stoves). Although you can learn these "on the fly" if you don't have them already, it's a good idea to practice these skills when you have the chance, either by working on some of your own household repairs or helping other people in your community who do hands-on work.

A wide variety of general hand tools are useful.

HAND-POWERED DRILLS can sometimes be found in secondhand stores or garage sales for very low prices. Larger-sized bits, such as spade-bits or (better yet) hole drills, are required for some of the water-treatment projects. Bits must be quite sharp to make drilling by hand more feasible.

HANDSAWS of multiple sizes for both wood and metal are useful as well. Secondhand wood saws are generally fairly dull, and even new saws will dull in time, so getting some sharpening files and learning how to use them properly is a good investment.

HAMMERS, NAILS, SCREWDRIVERS, AND SCREWS of many sizes should all be in your toolbox. Various sizes of nuts and bolts are very handy to have on hand for assembling and improvising. Other general woodworking implements, including measuring tapes, squares, and levels, are very useful for even the most basic projects.

Several of the projects (particularly the stoves) require the cutting, bending, or folding of metal. Even though this metal may be something as light and common as an aluminum food can, sharp edges can still be dangerous. This is especially true if the metal is under tension while being twisted. Be careful. Wear thick (ideally, leather) **GLOVES** to prevent cuts. Having the proper tools—such as a variety of **PLIERS AND SNIPS** for working with metal—will help prevent injuries.

SAFETY GOGGLES are a good idea when working with anything that might shear, shatter, or otherwise fling out bits of debris.

When I am improvising on a project, I often make use of one or more of the following generally handy materials:

- Baling twine (or any strong twine)

- Parachute cord (for projects requiring very strong cordage)

- Vapor barrier (or similar plastic sheets)

- Adhesives such as wood glue

- Duct tape (although this becomes gummy and fails with time, it can be useful if you are trying to set something up for the first time, or for temporary fixes)

Also, there are also several companies that specialize in hand-powered tools. Lehman's in the United States (www.Lehmans.com), and Lee Valley in Canada (www.LeeValley.com), have a wide selection of hand tools for wood-working and gardening, as well as other articles of interest. Both currently offer free catalogs upon request.

WATER

- Food-grade, covered containers of various sizes for potable water; bottles for transporting, and large containers like barrels for storage

Wells
- Digging tools, i.e., shovels and pickaxes
- Rope, pulley, tripod, and bucket for removing soil
- Rings or supports to keep well walls intact
- Chlorine (household bleach with no additives) for disinfecting well
- Windlass or hand-crank with bucket for raising water, or a hand-pump
- Materials to build cover and apron for well (or knowledge of how to use local materials, like rocks and clay, to make apron)
- Hydrological or topographical maps to help site the well

Rainwater Collection
- Appropriate roofing or collection surface (see page 8 for details)
- Collection gutter

- Downspout or tube for directing water to storage containers
- Food-grade storage container for water, either concrete (as in Figure 3c: Single-Tank Storage) or food-grade barrels. If barrels are used, drill and bit to make holes for spigot and connecting pipes, as well as plumbing coupling and fixtures and tubes (flexible tube can make it easier to adjust barrel placement)
- Plumber's tape for fixtures
- Caulking (and especially marine epoxy) are useful for patching leaks around fixtures on outside of barrels
- Window screen to cover intake or overflow pipes to prevent insect access
- Spigots or flow-control valves
- Hose or flexible tubing to help access water

Survival Sources
- For survival still: transparent plastic sheet, and can or small container
- For water from transpiration: transparent plastic bag and string or elastic tie

General Water Treatment
- Fine cotton cloth for straining water
- For chemical disinfection: household bleach (with no additives) or medical iodine, 2 percent USP strength

Solar Disinfection
- Small plastic bottles
- Black paint

Distillation
- For stovetop still: transparent plastic sheet and string or elastic tie with two pots
- Windows or large plastic sheets
- Black cloth for lightweight solar still
- Tubing or piping for continuous flow (if desired)
- General construction materials such as plywood, nails, etc.
- Black plastic for lining stills

Sand Filters
- Food-grade barrels
- Drill and bit to make holes for spigot and connecting pipes, as well as plumbing coupling and fixtures and tubes (flexible tube can make it easier to adjust barrel placement)
- Perforated metal plate the same size as bottom of the barrel
- Small stones or pot shards
- Fine sand
- Perforated pipe for water drainage
- Funnel and flexible hose or tube for filling filters
- Plumber's tape for fixtures
- Caulking (and especially marine epoxy) are again useful for patching leaks around fixtures on outside of barrels
- Spigots or flow-control valves

LATRINES AND GRAYWATER

Basic Latrines
- Shovels for digging holes
- Simple covering structure such as an outhouse, or materials for improvising that structure
- For ventilated improved pit latrine: ventilation pipe about 10 feet (3 meters) long and about 3 inches (7 cm) internal diameter

Composting Toilets
Jenkins Sawdust Toilet:
- Toilet seat and box or stand to elevate it
- Several 5-gallon buckets for receptacle
- Roughage (several options discussed on page 36)
- Compost bins outside can be made out of planking, shipping pallets, or other lumber (avoid pressure treated lumber, which will leach poisonous substances into your compost)

Two-Bin Latrine:
- Bricks, concrete, cinder blocks, or stone to build the foundation
- Outhouse or covering structure

COOL FOOD STORAGE

General
- Thermometer (ideally with high and low recording markers) to determine temperature of food storage locations
- Hygrometer to determine humidity
- Watertight, durable, reusable containers with tight-fitting lids for small food items
- Larger containers or baskets for vegetables and tubers (wooden crates with air circulation—or plastic milk crates—can be very useful)
- Cardboard boxes (especially with waxed coating for water resistance) are also useful and easy to get

Water Immersion
- Cage or perforated container to immerse in water
- Rope (and possibly stake) to prevent cage immersed in larger water body from floating away
- Containers with waterproof and tight-fitting lids

In-Ground Cooling
- Shovels for digging
- Bucket or crate with rope for use in "cold hole"
- Barrels for lining cold hole
- Containers for improvised root cellars, including garbage cans, barrels, freezers, or refrigerators (remember to have coolant and compressors removed)
- Insulation such as bales of hay, straw, Styrofoam, or even leaves
- Chicken wire or hardware cloth to keep rodents out
- Tarp to cover to cover straw or hay insulation

Cold Rooms, Cellars, or Icehouses
These structures require some carpentry or construction experience, and the exact materials needed will depend on your particular situation. General carpentry tools and materials are useful, with a definite emphasis on sufficient insulation and ventilation (either with screened vents in walls, or ventilation tubes).

Iceboxes:
- Insulated chest or container (a refrigerator could be used)
- Drainage tube and container for meltwater

Evaporative Cooling

- For bucket system: two buckets and a rope to use for hanging them
- For cabinet-style system: a chest or cabinet and a tray for water on top
- An absorbent large cloth or towel
- For pot-in-pot system: two pots, one larger than the other and unglazed; sand or soil to place between them; and a damp cloth on top

COOKING

General

- Matches and lighters
- Alternative fire-making devices (such as flint-and-steel) or skills (such as the ability to make a bow drill)
- Container or bucket for water to put out fires in an emergency
- Pots and cooking containers (black or black-painted for solar cookers)

Hayboxes

- Insulation, either solid or flexible, depending on type chosen (blankets, wool, cloth scraps, and aluminum foil can all be useful)
- An enclosure, either a box with a lid, or even a cloth bag or sack

Open Fires

- Hearth materials, if desired
- Small shovel or trowel if making a fire hole

Rocket Stove (and Variations)

- Sheet metal, aluminum cans, and metal pipes (as available)
- Tools for working and cutting metal safely: thick or leather gloves, pliers of several sizes, tin-snips, or other metal-cutting implements (such as hacksaws)
- Castable firebrick can increase stove efficiency and life span
- Fireproof insulation (see page 63)

For Dona Justa Stove

- Stovepipe or longer metal pipe for chimney
- Large metal sheet for stovetop and front plate
- Bricks or stone blocks for stove body (or skills to make cob or clay structures)

Solar Cookers

General reflector materials, including:

- Aluminum foil (heavy-duty varieties are more durable and can be worked without tearing as easily) in large amounts
- Corrugated cardboard (for backing)
- Glue or contact cement for attaching foil and cardboard
- Mirrors, aluminized Mylar, polished sheet metal, or other available highly reflective materials as appropriate
- Thermometers (such as in-stove type of thermometer for use in solar oven)

Simple Folding Solar Cooker

- Reflector
- Black pot
- Transparent plastic bag
- Wire rack or frame to elevate pot, or stiff wire with which to fashion a rack

Solar Oven

- Glass window
- Larger reflectors
- Housing materials such as plywood
- Insulation (such as alternating corrugated cardboard and aluminum foil)
- A pivoting mount or table can be useful for tracking the sun

Parabolic Cookers

- Cardboard, nail or tack, pencil, straight ruler and right-angle ruler, and scissors for drawing parabola and making parabolic template
- Large flexible reflector materials and backing appropriate for reflector (based on its strength and weight)
- Metal mounting pole or pipe

- Grill for cooker
- A pivoting mount or table can again be useful for tracking the sun

Conical Cooker
- Polished or reflective flexible metal sheet
- Large-diameter black pipe for water, or black metal sleeve for kettle
- Plywood disk and a metal mounting pole or pipe
- A pivoting mount or table can again be useful for tracking the sun

QUICK LIGHT AND HEAT

General Lighting
- A flashlight, especially a hand-cranked model, is very useful
- Reflectors and foil for concentrating light

Oil Lamp
- Oil or fat for fuel
- A heatproof container for fuel
- Wick (made out of commercial wicking material, frayed cotton rope, or other options as discussed on page 78)
- For Cresson Kearney's lamp, described on page 78, a glass mason jar, a wooden float, and wire

Candles
- Fat, tallow, or paraffin
- Wicks
- Mold for making candles (if desired)

Heat
- Wool clothing, extra blankets, and warm sleeping bags
- Plastic sheeting to cover windows and help retain heat

Peak Oil

Richard Heinberg's *The Party's Over: Oil, War, and The Fate of Industrial Societies* (New Society Publishers, 2003) is an excellent introduction to the topic of peak oil. In *Powerdown: Options and Actions for a Post-Carbon World* (New Society Publishers, 2004), Heinberg advocates specific strategies in response to the peak oil situation. His monthly newsletter is available at www.museletter.com.

Matthew David Savinar's book, *The Oil Age is Over: What to Expect as the World Runs Out of Cheap Oil, 2005–2050* (Self-Published, 2004) is another outstanding and readable introduction to the subject. There are also more articles and links at his website, www.lifeaftertheoilcrash.net.

Excellent websites on the subject of peak oil include: www.wolfatthedoor.org.uk, www.dieoff.org, www.hubbertpeak.com, and www.oilcrash.com.

Civilization and Industrialism

Derrick Jensen's writings are some of the most insightful, intelligent, moving, and relevant works I have ever read. I heartily encourage you to read his work, starting with *A Language Older than Words* (Chelsea Green Publishing, 2004) and his latest book, *Endgame*. Derrick Jensen's website at www.derrickjensen.org includes a subscription "reading club" where you can read other works in progress.

Anthropik.com posts discussions and essays about civilization and collapse. Check out the essential "The Thirty Theses."

Ran Prieur is a writer with keen and insightful analysis, essays, and commentary at RanPrieur.com.

Anthropologist Stanley Diamond wrote the excellent book titled *In Search of the Primitive: A Critique of Civilization* (Little, Brown & Company, 1966).

Chellis Glendinning's *My Name is Chellis and I'm in Recovery from Western Civilization* (Shambhala, 1994) is a moving book in which Glendinning examines her own childhood abuse and traces its roots to civilization itself. She offers commentary on the insanity of the dominant culture and ways in which indigenous cultures are sane.

Lewis Mumford (1895–1988) was an incredibly prolific writer, historian, and social critic. His books most relevant to the premises discussed in this book include the two-volume set *The Myth of the Machine, Volume I: Technics and Human Development* (1967) and *Volume II: The Pentagon of Power* (1974); and *The City in History: Its Origins, Its Transformations, and Its Prospects* (1968), all published by Harvest/HBJ Books.

John Zerzan has written several great books, including *Running on Emptiness: The Pathology of Civilization* (Feral House, 2002). He also edited the excellent anthology *Against Civilization: Readings and Reflections* (Feral House, 1999), which is available online at: http://www.blackandgreen.org/ac/index.html.

Daniel Quinn is the author of very readable novels about the origins of civilization: *Ishmael* (Bantam, 1992), *My Ishmael* (Bantam, 1998), and *The Story of B* (Bantam, 1997). I also recommend Daniel Quinn's website, www.ishmael.org.

Related writings by numerous authors are available at:
http://www.insurgentdesire.org.uk/
http://primitivism.com/

General Ecology and Overshoot

Overshoot: The Ecological Basis of Revolutionary Change by William R. Catton Jr. (University of Illinois Press, 1982) is a wonderful primer and introduction to the fundamentals of ecology and carrying capacity.

My website, inthewake.org, has more extensive listings and links on related subjects.

Page numbers in italics indicate illustrations.